*A Marriage after God's Own Heart*

A

*Marriage*

AFTER

*God's*

OWN

*Heart*

# DAVID CLARKE

Multnomah®Publishers *Sisters, Oregon*

A MARRIAGE AFTER GOD'S OWN HEART
published by Multnomah Publishers, Inc.

© 2001 by David E. Clarke, Ph.D., Inc.
International Standard Book Number: 1-57673-755-1

Cover image by VCG/Tony Stone Images

Scripture quotations are from:
*New American Standard Bible* © 1960, 1977 by the Lockman Foundation
Also quoted:
*The Holy Bible,* New International Version (NIV)
© 1973, 1984 by International Bible Society,
used by permission of Zondervan Publishing House

*Multnomah* is a trademark of Multnomah Publishers, Inc.,
and is registered in the U.S. Patent and Trademark Office.
The colophon is a trademark of Multnomah Publishers, Inc.

Printed in the United States of America

For information:
MULTNOMAH PUBLISHERS, INC.
POST OFFICE BOX 1720
SISTERS, OREGON 97759
Library of Congress Cataloging-in-Publication Data
Clarke, David, Ph. D.
A marriage after God's own heart / by David Clarke.
    p.cm.    ISBN 1-57673-755-1    1. Marriage—Religious aspects—
Christianity. 2. Spouses—Religious life. I. Title.
BV835.C575 2001    248.8'44—dc21    00-011430

04 05—10 9 8 7

# CONTENTS

# *Acknowledgments*

My deepest thanks to the following people, who contributed so much to the writing of this book:

Sandy Clarke, my precious soul mate. I cherish our oneness in Christ.

Emily, Leeann, Nancy, and William Clarke. I love each one of you very much. Your mom and I pray that each of you will marry someone with whom you can share Christ.

Bill and Kathleen Clarke, spiritual bonders from way back. You taught me how to love Jesus and walk with Him. Dad, a special thanks to you for all your editing.

Rocky Glisson, my true-blue friend and accountability partner.

Denise Hall, you're always there when I need you.

Ethel Harris, my secretary of twelve years, a woman of many talents, and one who knows all about spiritual intimacy. Your support and practical help are priceless to me.

Joyce Hart. There would be no book without you. Thanks for swinging the deal!

Betty Gasper. Thanks so much for your help with the revisions. You and your trusty fax machine saved the day!

Keith Wall, my editor at Multnomah Publishers. It was a pleasure to work with you. You made it a much better book.

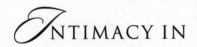

## Part One

Marriage

# 1

# MARRIAGE: THE IMPOSSIBLE DREAM?

*No Two People Can Make Marriage Work by Themselves*

*A*t one time or another, every couple has a house-guest—a relative, a friend, or someone you try to help. You and your spouse graciously decide to open your happy, comfortable home to this person for a brief stay. You are kind. You are caring. You are trying to meet a need. You are following the Bible's admonition to be hospitable.

You say to yourselves, "It's only for a little while. No big deal. It might even be fun. What could go wrong?" Your rose-colored, naive, unreasonably positive view of the situation is touching... and hopelessly inaccurate. The visit probably won't be "for a little while." It *is* a big deal. It won't be fun. Many things will go wrong. You are about to find out that you don't have the gift of hospitality.

Your experience as motel managers starts off pleasantly enough. Everybody is all smiles. You're helping a poor, dear, temporarily homeless person, and that gives you a warm feeling in your hearts. Your houseguest is grateful, humble, and considerate. For the first few days, maybe even the first week, things are fine.

"Make yourself at home.... What's ours is yours.... Thank

you.... You're welcome.... Sorry to be a bother.... Don't be silly—it's no bother."

But if your houseguest stays longer than a week (and most houseguests do), it begins to wear on you. Your beautiful, idyllic bed-and-breakfast (and lunch-and-dinner) inn quickly becomes a house of horrors. Your schedule is thrown off. Your carefully constructed routine is shot to pieces. You lose your personal space. You and your partner don't have time to talk. You realize that you have given control of your lives to an alien being.

You find yourselves in the middle of a hostage crisis, and you and your spouse are the hostages. You peek out the window, but there is no SWAT team out there to rescue you. No one is going to help. You're all alone now. Alone with your houseguest.

That...that...that...person is always around! Every time you turn around, you bump into your guest. The list of things you can't do in your own home is incredibly long. You can't drop your shoes in the middle of the living room. You can't wander into the kitchen in your striped pajamas. It suddenly dawns on you how stupid you look in your striped pajamas.

There isn't enough hot water for your shower. You can't sit in your favorite chair. Your houseguest has his selfish little hands on your television remote control! And—what a surprise—he doesn't like your favorite TV shows. You have to share the morning paper...and you hate to share. You reach for your special Snoopy glass...and it's not there.

You become desperate for the person to go. You make Xs on your wall calendar to count the days until your guest leaves. You begin giving him subtle hints that you want him to move on. You pack all his clothes and put the suitcase by the front door. You change the locks on the house. You leave an anonymous note on his pillow with this message:

If you don't leave by sundown tomorrow, something very bad will happen to you. This is not a joke.

The day finally comes when your houseguest leaves. You force a smile and mumble something about how much you enjoyed having him in your home. When you're certain he's gone, you and your spouse embrace passionately and shout for joy. The war is over, and you survived. Life will get back to normal. No more interruptions; no more interference. Just peace and stability. You even forget how stupid you look in your striped pajamas.

## A Different Kind of Houseguest

You have probably lived through the chaos and inconvenience of hosting a houseguest. No matter how much you care for the visitor, there is a limit to how long someone can be around, use your stuff, and upset your routine.

As hard as it may be to believe, it doesn't have to be this way. There is one person you can invite into your home who will bring peace and joy and intimacy. Can you imagine having a houseguest who will actually enhance your life and marriage? Think about a guest who helps to:

- ✦ improve your communication;
- ✦ create openness and vulnerability;
- ✦ deepen your commitment to each other;
- ✦ protect you from Satan's attacks.

There is such a houseguest. As you have probably guessed by now, I'm referring to Jesus Christ. When He comes to stay at your house, He removes burdens instead of creating them and makes you feel free, not trapped.

Over the past fifteen years, as a psychologist and speaker specializing in family issues, I have talked with hundreds of couples every year, both in my office and at my marriage seminars. Many of these couples try to make their marriages work by themselves, just the two of them, in their own power. I say to them: "Look, let's face reality. You can't do it on your own. You need help—supernatural help. You need Jesus Christ to be a permanent resident in your home, not just an occasional visitor."

## IS YOUR MARRIAGE AVERAGE OR AWESOME?

On a recent Sunday morning, I had just finished speaking on the importance of putting Jesus Christ at the center of marital relationships. After the worship service, I stayed at the front of the auditorium, and ten or twelve couples came up to talk with me. Two of these couples stand out in my mind.

All four spouses knew Jesus Christ personally. Both couples attended church faithfully. Both couples had been married about the same length of time. But that's where the similarities ended. The contrast between their two marriages was startling—and revealing.

The first couple told me that God had blessed them with many gifts. They had stable jobs, a nice home, great kids, good health, and a real love for Jesus. But, they told me sadly, they weren't really happy in their marriage. They still loved each other, but there was no passion or excitement anymore. The fire that had blazed in the early years of their relationship had long since gone out. Though they weren't going to split up, they were tired of trudging along in a dull, predictable, ho-hum relationship. Their life together was all right, but their marriage had no particular meaning or purpose.

The second couple approached me, and before they even opened their mouths, I knew that there was something different about them. They held hands and smiled at each other. Their eyes sparkled. They exuded an energy that was hard to describe. They told me that up until a year and half ago, their marriage had been pretty boring and uninspiring. At best, their relationship could be categorized as *average*. Then they faced some painful events and turned to Jesus for help. They leaned on Him, sought His will, and, most of all, reconnected to Him as a couple. He got them through their crises, and they decided to continue including Him in their relationship.

They told me that Jesus had transformed their average marriage into an awesome one. They'd gone from a tedious treadmill kind of relationship to an exciting, unpredictable adventure. They were growing together spiritually, serving Jesus as a team, and making a difference in the world. Along the way, they had developed a much deeper level of spiritual, emotional, and sexual intimacy.

So let me ask you: Which kind of marriage do you want to have? Do you want a lackluster, mediocre marriage like that of the first couple I described? That's the kind of marriage many—perhaps most—couples have. It's not awful, but it's not very good either. Or do you want an intimate, fulfilling connection like the second couple enjoyed? I know your answer. The second kind of marriage is the relationship you've always wanted. The truth is that you can experience the kind of closeness most spouses only dream about. And the only way to get this kind of vibrant, exceptional marriage is through Jesus Christ.

Picture yourselves bringing Jesus into your home to live with you. He'll be more than a houseguest; He'll become a permanent addition to your marriage. He'll be the third member of your relationship. When Jesus is involved, three isn't a crowd. Three is just right!

And when you have Jesus Christ with you, you also have God the Father and the Holy Spirit. It's a package deal! Can you imagine having all the power, guidance, and love of the Godhead in your marriage? Well, you *can* have it. God wants you to have it. He's waiting for you to invite Him into your home.

The presence of God through His Son, Jesus Christ, is what every marriage needs. If you let Him, God will give you the relationship you've always longed to experience. Yours can become a marriage after God's own heart. He will take a *good* marriage and make it *great*. He will take a struggling marriage and get it back on track. He will take a dead marriage and bring it back to life.

## REALITY CHECK

I've got good news and bad news about marriage. Let's start with the bad news. The whole idea of marriage is insane. It makes no sense. Marriage expects two people to live together in harmony and intimacy, but the two are:

+ different sexually,
+ different physically,
+ different hormonally,
+ different intellectually,
+ different in brain construction and chemistry,
+ different in emotional expression,
+ different in personality,
+ different in family background.

To top it all off, both are selfish. This is nothing less than a recipe for disaster! The divorce rate of 50 percent in the United States doesn't surprise me. In fact, I'm surprised it isn't higher. When you consider the enormous challenges of marriage and the enormous differences between men and women, I'm amazed that the divorce rate isn't 80 or 90 percent.

Marriage is the one human relationship with the greatest potential for conflict. Just think about it. The husband won't talk; the wife won't stop talking. He can't remember anything that happened more than ten minutes ago; she remembers everything that ever happened to her ("I remember coming down the birth canal. It was dark, and I felt cramped. I heard screaming and moaning. Suddenly, it was very bright, and I could see for the first time. The doctor was a small man with a cheesy-looking goatee and bad breath. The wallpaper had a rocking chair print, red and navy blue…and out the window I could see….") Even if the husband could remember his birth, he wouldn't want to talk about it.

The wife wants to describe, in excruciating detail, every event of her day. And she wants her husband to listen and show interest in her monologue. She'll spend forty-five minutes talking about an event that lasted only five minutes. The husband will sum up his entire day with just one word: "Okay" or "Fine" or "Good."

He is a logical, black-and-white thinker who keeps his emotions buried inside. She is a sensitive, touchy-feely soul who shares her emotions easily and spontaneously. He didn't cry when his fifteen-year-old dog died. She cries when she sees a dead squirrel—one she doesn't even know—on the road.

She's happy having sex once a week. He'd like sex four times a week. She wants to "snuggle" and "cuddle." He wants sex. She wants to have a deep, personal conversation. He wants sex. She wants a romantic, subtle buildup to sex. His idea of a subtle buildup to sex is pinching her on the bottom and saying, "How about it, baby?"

He likes movies with plenty of gunfights, explosions, bodies in the streets, and high-tech special effects. His movies don't contain much in the way of complicated, sophisticated conversations. Most of the dialogue goes like this: "I'm gonna kill you, sucka!" She prefers movies filled with romance, relationships, and people talking about romance and relationships. She doesn't like to see movie characters die violent deaths for no good reason. But it is okay if someone dies after a long illness and has spent two hours talking about death and how hard it is to leave a cherished lover. She's watched the six-volume set of *Pride and Prejudice* fifteen times and says it gets better every time she sees it. Sound familiar?

As I said, on your own, marriage is impossible. That's the most important truth about marriage. It's not just really, really difficult—not just a tremendous challenge. It's impossible. Marriage is a never-ending series of conflicts, misunderstandings, and mind-boggling missed connections.

## WHY ARE WE SO DIFFERENT?

Why did God make men and women so unbelievably different? The main reason is so that we would have to depend on Him. God wants to be at the center of every marriage, so He made the relationship so difficult that we have to keep Him there to make it work. That's just like God, isn't it? He makes sure that He is the answer to all of life's problems.

Without God's presence and power, there isn't a couple alive that can build a truly intimate, deep love. Oh, you can stay together and limp along without God. Lots of couples— Christians and non-Christians—do that. It might be a decent marriage, a stable marriage. Nobody's going to leave. You're staying together—not because you're passionately in love, but out of obligation—because it's the right thing to do or because you have children and you don't want to break up the family.

Of course, staying together *is* the right thing for couples to do. But it's not the right thing to stay together *like that*. If you do, you're settling for far less than what God wants for your marriage. That kind of grind-it-out marriage is not what He has in mind for you.

I ask all the limp-along couples I meet the same question: "How is your marriage going?" I always get the same answer: "Oh, okay. Good. All right. Things could be worse." Okay? Pretty good? All right? Things could be worse? What kind of marriage is that? It's the kind you get when you exclude God from your day-to-day life as a couple.

## THE GOOD NEWS

Now for the good news: Marriage is the one human relationship with the greatest potential for intimacy. Even with all our differences, marriage can work beautifully when we keep God at the center of the relationship.

God wants marriage to be a glorious, passionate, deeply intimate, sacred, and magnificent love relationship. He wants us to
connect in communication, to be best friends, to meet each
other's real needs, to have fun, and to glorify Him in our love.

Do you want to read one of the most beautiful and moving
descriptions of love ever written? You'd better be sitting down
when you read this passage from Scripture because it might
knock you off your feet:

> Put me like a seal over your heart,
> Like a seal on your arm.
> For love is as strong as death,
> Jealousy is as severe as Sheol;
> Its flashes are flashes of fire,
> The very flame of the Lord.
> Many waters cannot quench love,
> Nor will rivers overflow it;
> If a man were to give all the riches of his house for love,
> It would be utterly despised. (Song of Solomon 8:6–7)

Whoa! Now that's real love—a love that is a fire, an eternal
flame that oceans of water cannot extinguish. When you read
these verses, you can feel its passion, power, and intensity. You
can have this wonderful kind of love in your marriage. God
wants you to experience it in your relationship, and He will give
it to you if you will give Him the chance.

## THE ROAD AHEAD

All of this raises a big question: How do you get there? How do
you bring Jesus, God, and the Holy Spirit into your relationship?
How do you allow God to give you the passion and deep connection you're missing? I'm going to show you how in the following chapters.

In part 1, I explain the importance of spiritual intimacy in marriage. Physical and emotional intimacy are important, but they're not enough. Spiritual intimacy is what you must have to achieve God's best in your marriage.

In part 2, I cover the five major benefits of spiritual intimacy in marriage: an exhilarating ride for two, great sex, deep communication, protection from the marriage killers, and a bottomless reservoir of fuel for the marriage journey. When you read about these benefits, you'll want them. Once you and your spouse have them, your marriage will never be the same.

In part 3, I get down to the nitty-gritty. I show you in a specific, practical, step-by-step fashion how to cultivate the presence of God as a couple by consistently bringing God into seven critical areas of your relationship: prayer, Bible reading, spiritual conversations, worship, accountability, service, and depending on Him in the tough times.

Finally, in part 4, I describe the major barriers to spiritual intimacy and how to overcome them. I present ten ways to motivate your mate to spiritually bond, and I challenge the six main excuses most people use to avoid spiritual intimacy.

When you've finished this book, you'll know how to spiritually bond as a man and a woman. You'll be able to develop the kind of forever love that God intends for you to enjoy.

# 2

# A FLIMSY
# FOUNDATION

-~~⊙~~-

*Physical Intimacy Is Not Enough*

bout four years ago, my wife, Sandy, and I hit a wall in our marriage. At that point, we had been married for fourteen years, and we were still happy together, still in love, still doing well. But we realized that our relationship had reached a plateau. We admitted to each other, reluctantly, that we had begun to coast a little. Our life together had become too predictable, comfortable, and routine. We agreed that we were too young to be an old, boring, married couple!

Sandy and I were not satisfied with where we were. An "okay" marriage wasn't enough for us. We wanted more. We wanted to get to the next level—a deeper level. We wanted more intimate communication, more playfulness, and better sex. But we weren't sure exactly what was missing. We didn't know what we needed to do to get past the barrier between us and a closer bond.

We began to search for the reason our relationship was stalled. We spent a great deal of time looking for the missing piece. We evaluated; we talked; we prayed. It's embarrassing to confess that it took us several years to figure it out. It's embarrassing because the solution had been there all along—right in front of us. We already possessed it.

What was the one thing that could energize our marriage and take us where we wanted to go? It was a relationship with Jesus.

Many couples today are in the same situation that Sandy and I were in four years ago. Their relationships are suffering—and in some cases, dying—even as they have within reach the one thing that would save them and make all the difference.

What if I told you that there is a way to build intimacy—real intimacy—with a member of the opposite sex? What if I told you that there is a way to improve every single area of your relationship? What if I told you that there is a way to avoid serious mistakes in your relationship—mistakes that cripple and scar? What if I told you that there is a way to put the power of God Himself to work in your relationship? You'd want it, wouldn't you? Of course you would! Well, there is a way to achieve these goals, and it is within your reach.

## ONE FLESH

You might be thinking, *Yeah, right. Come on, Dave! This sounds too good to be true.* Sure, it sounds too good to be true—but it is true. There is a way to create a relationship this good—a deeply intimate, strong, safe relationship powered by God Himself.

God wants us to have this kind of marriage so much that He didn't waste any time bringing it to our attention. In Genesis 2, we find the first—and in many ways the most important—message in the Bible about male-female intimacy. In it, God describes the relationship He wants every married couple to enjoy:

> For this cause a man shall leave his father and his mother and shall cleave to his wife; and they shall become one flesh. (Genesis 2:24)

The words *one flesh* are, very simply, God's definition of heterosexual intimacy. And if it's God's definition, it must be the best one.

When Jesus Christ was asked about marriage, He referred to this same one-flesh relationship:

> And He answered and said, "Have you not read, that He who created them from the beginning made them male and female, and said, 'For this cause a man shall leave his father and his mother, and shall cleave to his wife; and the two shall become one flesh'? Consequently they are no longer two, but one flesh. What therefore God has joined together, let no man separate." (Matthew 19:4–6)

When the apostle Paul spoke about man-woman relationships, he also referred to married couples being one flesh (1 Corinthians 6:16; Ephesians 5:31). Now, I don't know about you, but when both Jesus and Paul use the same concept to describe marriage, it gets my attention.

What does it mean to be one flesh? It is a complete coming together of a man and a woman in three vital areas:

- physical,
- emotional,
- spiritual.

God says that you have true, complete intimacy only when you are bonded in all three areas.

Which of these three areas is the most important in a relationship? Which component of intimacy provides the best foundation for a relationship? Your answer will determine the success or the failure of your marriage.

## LET'S GET PHYSICAL

We all know that American culture is obsessed with sex. In every form of media, sex is on center stage. You can hardly find a movie without offensive, erotic language, nudity, and sexual intercourse, either explicit or implied. Just about every show on television—sitcoms, dramas, talk shows—is sexually oriented. If the actors aren't having sex, they're talking about it. Even nature shows seem to be showing more sex. I really don't want to see, up close and in color, the mating dance and intercourse of the black mountain gorilla.

If you do happen to find a television show worth watching, the commercials bombard you with sex. Companies use sex to sell everything from cars to vacuum cleaners to beer. You may have seen the extremely attractive and scantily clad models parading around in the ads for a famous lingerie company. Is this necessary? Or how about the lady in the shower who seems to be having an orgasm as she uses a certain type of shampoo? This isn't funny—it's nasty.

Walk into a bookstore or grocery store and just glance at the rows and rows of magazines. On just about every cover, you'll see an unbelievably thin, airbrushed beauty who forgot to put on enough clothes. Most magazines targeted to men and women (even teenagers) contain articles on how to improve your sex life. There's always some amazing breakthrough in sexual technique guaranteed to get you the sex you want and deserve.

You're not even safe reading the sports section of your local newspaper. Right there under the box scores and batting averages, you might find a huge ad for massage parlors or men's clubs. Suggestive sexual messages and pictures of seductive women appear next to the story about last night's big game.

What's more, the Internet has made every type of pornography accessible to anyone with a computer and a modem. And believe me, millions of men and boys are accessing it. Typically, guys go for the visual pornography, while women, searching for a meaningful relationship, are drawn to chat rooms. Satan is using sex on the Web to destroy millions of lives and relationships.

Through all these media outlets, we receive the message loud and clear: "Get all the sex you can with a variety of partners. Don't limit yourself to sex with your spouse. That's hopelessly old-fashioned. Sex outside of marriage is more exciting. The kinkier the sex, the better. When you meet someone new, have sex as soon as you can because sexual compatibility is critical. Just be careful out there, will you? Use protection and practice safe sex. We don't want you picking up some disease."

That's our society's view of sex. It's also Satan's view. Now let's look at the truth about sex—God's truth.

## HOW FAR WILL SEX TAKE YOU?

Can you base a relationship on sexual intimacy? Yes, you can. Is it a good idea? No, it is not. A relationship based solely on the physical will last six months to a year and a half. Let's face it: Human beings quickly grow bored with anything familiar and common. As powerful as it can be, sexual attraction alone is not enough to sustain a relationship. When you've seen the same naked body twenty, fifty, or two hundred times, you know that not much is going to change. It may be a beautiful body, and you may be attracted to it, but you cannot continue to depend only on that body for intimacy.

Every major newspaper every day of the week proves that this is true. Just look at the personality/celebrity column in the entertainment or lifestyle section of the paper. You'll find sad stories about the oh-so-brief relationships of Hollywood stars. As I travel the country speaking, I read these entertainment columns faithfully (just for research purposes, of course), and I find the same old story hundreds of times over. Two beautiful Hollywood actors begin a relationship. They might get married, or they might not. They might have kids, or they might not. It doesn't make any difference, because their relationship won't last long whether they choose a traditional family structure or not. Within a year I'll most likely read that the famous couple has broken up. Usually, each finds a new partner very quickly.

What happens to these celebrities? They usually base their relationships on sex. All they have is two beautiful bodies and nothing else. Their physical relationship may be tremendous for a while. But when the sex runs out of steam, so do they. They have to move on to the next beautiful body.

Sex, whether inside or outside marriage, cannot carry a relationship far under its own power. Premarital sex and extramarital sex are incredibly intense, passionate, and exciting. I've talked to many couples who have described the thrilling rush of sex outside of marriage. Of course, the catch is that it is a very brief and tremendously destructive experience. The temporary pleasure runs out, and the individuals are left trying to pick up the shattered pieces of their lives.

Sex inside marriage is morally pure and part of God's plan. It also can be intense, passionate, exciting, and fun. But it still can't carry a relationship very far. Even if you remain faithful to your marriage partner and your sexual relationship keeps getting better, it alone cannot lead to a long and intimate life together. The love of many couples dies just a few short years after they marry. Why? Because their foundation was physical attraction and sex.

Let's be honest. Many of you can admit, from personal experience, that sex alone isn't enough. Like many of my clients, you'd tell me: "Dave, I've had several relationships based strictly on sex, and they didn't last." My response is: "Of course they didn't last. Though sex is an important part of marriage, God never designed it to carry a relationship forty or fifty years."

The bottom line is this: God created sex to be an enjoyable and a meaningful part of marriage, but He never intended it to be the *most important* aspect of a couple's relationship.

# 3

# "I DON'T LOVE YOU ANYMORE"

*Emotional Intimacy Is Not Enough*

Have you noticed the proliferation of "love experts" in our society? These men and women have devoted their lives to helping couples experience real, lasting intimacy. They really, really want you to be happy in your love relationships. And, of course, they really, really want you to buy all their products so *they* can be happy.

These experts dispense their advice through every possible media. If you walk into a bookstore, you'll see their books on the bestseller shelves. If you turn on your television, you'll see them on talk shows, the evening news, news magazine shows, and public television. They're on the radio. They have web sites. They're in newspapers and popular magazines. They even have their own infomercials to sell videos and audiotapes containing all their secrets about love.

It's very easy to be impressed with these love specialists. Looking at them and listening to them talk makes you want to believe them. They are attractive, articulate, and successful. They have advanced degrees (not always in psychology, but let's not be picky). And they certainly seem like nice people. They smile a lot, they have big teeth, and they exude warmth and kindness.

These love doctors have a wide variety of creative solutions to all the problems men and women face in relationships. They teach you how to understand male-female differences, how to locate and comfort your inner child, how to communicate on many different levels, how to resolve conflict, how to keep romance in your marriage, and, of course, how to have exhilarating, fabulous, erotic sex every time you hit the bed.

There's just one tiny problem with these experts' carefully constructed marriage enrichment programs. Their advice frequently doesn't work in *their own marriages*. Many well-known media love doctors have been divorced—often more than once. Now, I'm not criticizing them for being divorced. But most divorced people don't set themselves up as experts on marriage.

Why haven't these experts been able to use their relationship techniques to save their own marriages? It's not because their ideas are terrible. In fact, they have some good ideas. It's because their advice is usually limited to just two areas of love. They base everything they say about marriage on emotional and sexual love. Although they try as hard as they can to keep the feeling of love going in their relationships, they can't do it, and they can't help you do it either.

Those who approach love and relationships without a biblically based perspective are shortsighted at best and totally blind at worse. All they have to go on are human wisdom and strategies. They don't know God, so have no idea what *He* can do for a marriage. Emotional love is all they can see.

## IS EMOTIONAL INTIMACY A GOOD FOUNDATION?

Can you base a relationship on emotional intimacy? Yes, you can. That's what these love doctors recommend doing. Is this a good idea? No, it is not. A relationship based solely on emotional intimacy will last four to seven years. That's better than the six months to a year and a half you get with a relationship based on sex, but it's still not very long.

Your feelings of love and care for your partner come and go. Haven't you noticed? Even if you work hard at communicating, handling conflict, and understanding male-female differences, there are still times when you don't *feel* in love with your spouse. As the years go by, you can lose more and more of those feelings. One day you might wake up and discover that they are completely gone.

If you choose to base your marriage on emotional intimacy only, you're doomed to end up in one of two situations. I'll describe both by telling about two couples I met recently.

### "We Just Kept Drifting Apart"

It's my first session with this couple. Ten minutes into the hour, I already know their story. It's one I've heard far too many times to count. The wife tells their tale:

> We fell in love and got married. That was twelve years ago now. Boy, how time flies! The first few years were great. We were deeply in love. Crazy about each other. We had a lot of things in common, could talk for hours, and sex was terrific. Everything was so new, fresh, and exciting. I couldn't wait to see Bill every day. To talk to him, to touch him, just to be with him.
>
> Then we had the two kids, and life just kept getting busier. Life settled into a routine, and it wasn't as much fun being together. I think it was around our seventh year of marriage when we both noticed that things had changed between us. We were comfortable together. Content. Secure. But not passionate. It was as though we'd lost our spark and couldn't get it back again.
>
> We tried to turn things around by reading some marriage books, going to a marriage retreat, and seeing

our pastor for a few hours of counseling. We read a book on sex. I even bought a set of videotapes from a psychologist I saw on an infomercial.

But nothing helped. We just kept drifting apart, leading lives that were more and more separate. Now, we don't have much feeling between us. We still love each other, but it's a brother-sister kind of love. We're not *in love*, and we miss that. We care about each other, and we're staying together no matter what...but we wonder if we can get our passion back.

Sound familiar? So many couples end up just like this one. Their love, once so alive and intense, slowly drains away until there's nothing left except commitment, duty, and security. It's a slow, agonizing way to kill a marriage. A good title for a movie about this kind of marital decay would be *Dead Couple Walking*. I tell this couple that they are boring each other to death and that they need to stop it. I say that what has happened to them is painful, but not unusual. I tell them that there is a way to bring back the passion, to reignite their love. I assure them that with God's help and with hard work, that's what we're going to do.

## "I WANT A DIVORCE"

I'm sitting with another couple in our first session together. They tell me another story I have heard many times. This time, it's the husband who does the talking:

I just don't love Debbie anymore. My feelings are gone. Totally gone. And I can't see any way in the world to get them back. I used to love her—at least I think I did. We had some good times. She's a good person, and I care about her. But the more I think about it, the more I wonder if I really ever loved her at all.

We were so young when we got married. What do

you know when you're just twenty-two? Looking back, I realize that I never should have married her. We're two very different people.

It's not you, Debbie. It's me. I've changed. I'm different. I feel trapped in our marriage. I'm not happy. It'll just hurt you and the kids if I stay in this dead, miserable marriage. I've got to get out and start over. I want to be happy again. I've thought a lot about this, and I've come to a decision. I want a divorce.

Debbie is devastated, in shock. She tells me that she had no idea this bombshell was coming. She's still in love with her husband, but he has no feelings for her at all.

Debbie's going to have to get ready for another bombshell: It's very likely that he's already found someone else he thinks he's in love with.

I tell this couple that their emotional intimacy has run out. At least, *his* has run out. There's no doubt that their love is stone-cold dead. Nevertheless, I tell them that there is a way to bring it back from the dead. There is a way to reenergize his love and create a brand-new relationship. Their love can be better than it ever was.

Please believe me when I tell you that a marriage based on emotional intimacy will end up one of these two ways. It's not just a possibility; it's inevitable. Keep in mind that being a Christian couple and attending church regularly is no protection. I've heard stories like these from many Christians. They went to church faithfully. They went to Sunday school. They tithed. They even had positions of leadership in their churches. And their love still ran dry.

I don't have to work too hard to convince you that emotional intimacy alone can't sustain a marriage, do I? I'm sure that many of you reading this can relate to these two sad stories. If we could talk about it, you might tell me: "Dave, you're right. In my previous marriage, we loved each other, and we worked at the relationship.

But we lost our love." Or you might confide, "You know, my husband [or wife] and I have had a bland, mediocre, lifeless marriage for a long time. Oh, we're committed to staying together, but neither of us thinks our relationship will improve." My response to both statements would be: "I'm not surprised. God never designed emotional intimacy to carry a relationship forty or fifty years. It can't do that on its own."

Like these two couples and thousands of other couples I've worked with, you may be asking, "What can we do when our love dies?" There's only one thing you can do—learn and implement the secret to *genuine* intimacy.

# THE SECRET TO GENUINE INTIMACY

*The Glue That Bonds Couples Together for a Lifetime*

hat's quite a chapter title, isn't it? You're probably wondering how in the world I can claim to know the secret of genuine intimacy. Haven't psychologists, philosophers, authors, and all kinds of relationship experts been searching for this secret for generations? Yes, they have. The problem is that they've been searching in all the wrong places.

The secret to success in every area of life, including relationships with the opposite sex, comes from God and His Word. The secret—God's secret—to having a fulfilling, exhilarating, lasting marriage is spiritual intimacy. Can you base a relationship on spiritual intimacy? Of course you can. A marriage based on spiritual intimacy can last a lifetime.

Strong words, but true words. The spiritual is the most important part of us as individuals. We are spiritual beings above all else. That's how God created us. The spiritual, therefore, must also be the most important part of our relationship with the opposite sex.

A large part of my love for Sandy comes from God and the

connection we share in Him. On my own, in human strength, I can't love her deeply or consistently, not just because it's so hard to live with someone twenty-four hours a day, seven days a week (although that certainly is true), but because I need God's help to love her.

## AN EPHESIANS 5:25 KIND OF LOVE

How can I love Sandy the way Ephesians 5:25 commands me to love her? Just read this verse: "Husbands, love your wives, just as Christ also loved the church and gave Himself up for her." Wow! That verse takes my breath away every time I read it. Do you realize what it's saying? This is nothing less than the highest possible standard of love—the ultimate in sacrificial love. Christ gave everything to the church. He gave His life!

I'm supposed to love Sandy like Christ loved the church? You must be kidding! When people look at how I treat Sandy, their first thought ought to be: *You know, looking at Dave and Sandy, I can't help but picture Christ's unconditional, sacrificial love for the church.* I'm sure this happens all the time…in my dreams.

I just can't love Sandy like this in my own power. Like a lot of men, I'm selfish. I do love Sandy, but I have a terrible habit of thinking of my needs first. I'll confess two areas in which I've been known to be just a tad bit self-centered: food and sex.

Satisfying my need for food is very important to me. I think about dinner all day long. You've heard that little piece of advice doctors and nutritionists like to use to make you feel guilty: eat like a king at breakfast, a prince at lunch, and a pauper at dinner. That's one of the dumbest things I've ever heard. If you want to be miserable, go ahead and try it. I'm not hungry at the crack of dawn. Lunch is lunch—a quick sandwich or leftovers. Big deal. Ah, but dinner…. Dinner is the culinary centerpiece of my day.

Most mornings, I call Sandy from my office to ask what we're having for dinner that evening. If she's not decided yet, I get a little on edge. My whole day depends on a fabulous dinner, and she's not sure what we're going to eat? At lunchtime, I call her again. By this time, she usually has an answer. I spend the rest of the day dreaming about dinner and how delicious it's going to be.

At least several times during the day I tell Sandy, "Make sure we have enough food." One of the greatest fears of the Clarke men is that there won't be enough food for dinner. One of our ancestors must have slowly starved to death. Of course, this fear may have something to do with watching my four kids descend on the dinner table like a pack of hyenas feeding at the kill.

If I'm not thinking about food, I'm thinking about sex. I like sex, and I like to have it when *I* want to have it. I don't automatically and naturally consider whether it's a convenient time for Sandy. Her schedule, her stress load, and her frame of mind usually don't enter the equation.

It's amazing how powerful my sex drive can be. Sandy can be in bed, sick as a dog. She's rocking back and forth, moaning in pain. She clutches a tissue box to her chest, and the air reeks of menthol cough drops. I sit down by her on the bed and gently say: "Too bad you feel sick, honey. But I've got something to make you feel better." I don't know why she gets so angry. I'm only trying to help.

As you can see, I can be a selfish guy. I admit it. I can't, in my own power, get myself out of the way and focus on Sandy and her needs.

## A 1 Corinthians 13 Kind of Love

As if Ephesians 5:25 weren't demanding enough, we have to live up to 1 Corinthians 13. This is the all-time classic Bible passage on love. We come across it everywhere we turn: in greeting cards, in books, in magazines, in sermons, and on plaques. I think it is the world's most beautiful, moving, and familiar piece of writing on the many attributes of love.

There's just one catch. No one can love this way! The kind of love described in this marvelous chapter of the Bible is so far

beyond the capability of the typical couple that it's not even real-
istic. Read these verses carefully and slowly, and then tell me if
I'm right or not:

> Love is patient, love is kind, and is not jealous; love does
> not brag and is not arrogant, does not act unbecomingly;
> it does not seek its own, is not provoked, does not take
> into account a wrong suffered, does not rejoice in
> unrighteousness, but rejoices with the truth; bears all
> things, believes all things, hopes all things, endures all
> things. Love never fails. (1 Corinthians 13:4–8)

See what I mean? By nature, human beings exhibit love that
is often the exact opposite of the kind described in these verses.
Name one couple—just one—who can consistently love in all
these ways in their human strength. I thought so. No one is this
nice! No one is this gracious! In my line of work, I've met some
of the nicest people in the world—sweet, caring, considerate, and
willing to do anything to help you. Saints! But not one of these
supernice individuals could maintain a 1 Corinthians 13 love for
his or her spouse for even one full day. No way!

As you may have guessed already, Sandy is a lot nicer than I
am. But she's not perfect. I won't go into great detail, because she's
reading these pages as I write them, and I really want to live to
finish the book. I will, however, give you one small example of
her lack of 1 Corinthians 13 kind of love.

I wear the most practical, protective, and affordable sunglasses available in America. Many men feel compelled to buy
those expensive, stylish sunglasses that everyone considers cool.
Not me. I'm a simple man with simple tastes. My sunglasses have
huge, square, wraparound lenses, and sell for $9.95 at the drug-
store. They're so big that they fit nicely over my regular glasses.
If one of my kids breaks them, no problem. They snap right back
together. I love my sunglasses.

There is, however, a drawback to wearing sunglasses like these: a distinct, easily identifiable group of individuals prefers the same kind, namely, eighty-year-old men who have had cataract surgery. In fact, I have noticed that many older, retired people here in Florida wear sunglasses like mine. That doesn't bother me. I figure these elderly folks, in their accumulated wisdom and experience, have decided that these particular sunglasses are the best.

My choice of sunglasses seems to amuse Sandy. She thinks they are hopelessly stodgy and, frankly, goofy-looking. She continually makes snide comments about how my sunglasses make me look like an old man ready for a rest home. When I turned forty a while back, she increased her petty attacks:

"Can I help you walk up these steps?"

"Would you like a shawl for your bony little knees?"

"Shall I pick up some Geritol for you?"

The woman is merciless, just merciless. Of course, she wears ritzy, trendy sunglasses, and that makes her think she's better than I am.

Some time ago, I drove Sandy and our five-year-old son, William, to pick up our three daughters at school. I was wearing my sunglasses, and as we were waiting in line with a number of other cars, a friend of Sandy's pulled alongside our van and motioned for me to roll down my window. When I did, she leaned out her window and said in a concerned voice, "I didn't know you had eye surgery, Dave! How did it go?"

Sandy began laughing hysterically and couldn't stop. Over the next several weeks she told this story to all our friends. Was this nice? Was this kind? Was this 1 Corinthians 13 in action? I don't think so.

These examples of how Sandy and I have failed to fulfill Ephesians 5:25 and 1 Corinthians 13 are humorous, I hope, and not all that serious. But when we as married couples fall short of God's definition of love, it can be very serious and not at all funny.

It can get ugly. Many relationships unravel amid unresolved conflicts, bitterness, angry and hurtful exchanges, coldness, affairs, and divorce.

## GOD IS LOVE, AND DON'T FORGET IT

Since we can't love each other the way God wants us to in our own power, what can we do? How can we experience true love? God provides the answer:

> Beloved, let us love one another, for love is from God; and everyone who loves is born of God and knows God. The one who does not love does not know God, for God is love. (1 John 4:7–8)

That pretty much clears it up, doesn't it? If you had any doubt where true love comes from, here's your answer. God is love, and all genuine love comes from Him. The love described in Ephesians 5:25 and 1 Corinthians 13 isn't human love! It's God's love! Even Christians, who ought to know better, often forget this simple yet profound truth. And when we forget it, our love becomes an extremely limited, human love. That kind of love doesn't last long.

## SPIRITUAL BONDING

If you want to love each other with God's love, you must be connected to Him as a couple. You must join spiritually. The secret to genuine, lasting intimacy in a relationship is becoming one flesh, spiritually. I call this *spiritual bonding*.

Spiritual bonding is consistently placing God at the center of your relationship and growing ever closer to Him as a couple. This means that you include God in everything—you invite Him into every nook and cranny of your relationship. It means that your souls come together in the pursuit of God. It is sharing Christ. It is tapping the power of the Holy Spirit and putting Him to work in your relationship. It is, without question, the deepest form of intimacy available to a man and a woman.

When you spiritually bond, it is no longer the two of you who do the loving. It is God Himself who does the loving. My marriage is not just a matter of me trying to love Sandy; it's a matter of *God* loving Sandy through me. It's not just a matter of Sandy trying to love me; it's a matter of God loving me through Sandy. Our love will never fail because it flows from our precious heavenly Father.

So far, I've talked in a general way about the importance of spiritual intimacy in a love relationship. In the next five chapters, we'll examine the *specific benefits* you as a couple will receive as a result of spiritual bonding.

PART TWO

THE

BENEFITS OF

SPIRITUAL

INTIMACY

# 5

# TAKE THE RIDE
# OF YOUR LIVES!

~~⟨ౚ⟩~~

*The First Benefit: Exhilarating Closeness*

I had always wanted to ride one of the famous San Francisco cable cars. It seemed like such an exciting and romantic thing to do. Humphrey Bogart, my favorite movie actor, rode a cable car in the classic movie *Dark Passage*. Humphrey looked incredibly cool on this ride—a little tense, but cool. The wind whipped his thinning hair. He had steely eyes and a little smirk that said, "I'm Humphrey Bogart, and you're not." Of course, Bogie would've looked cool waiting in line at the post office.

I could just picture my one true love, Sandy, and me swinging up onto a cable car. I'd give her my best Bogie smirk, and she'd say in a low, throaty voice: "Dave, you remind me of Humphrey Bogart—just taller, better looking, and with more hair." I'd reply, "Yeah, baby, I know. Here's looking at you, kid." And together, we'd rumble up and down the beautiful hills of San Francisco on that cable car.

Okay, it was a crazy fantasy. But it was *my* fantasy, and I liked it.

Recently, my cable car dream finally came true. Mark Calcagno, a good friend who pastors a church outside Oakland, flew Sandy and me there so I could conduct a weekend seminar for his parishioners. I was looking forward to speaking at the church, but I must admit that my first thought was: *I'm going to ride a cable car!* And, sure enough, that's what we did.

On Saturday afternoon, following two talks on parenting, Sandy and I drove across the Bay to San Francisco. We grabbed a loaf of sourdough bread at Fisherman's Wharf and made a bee-line for the cable car depot. After waiting in line for an hour and a half, Bogie (that's me) and his babe boarded the cable car.

Since it was crowded, there were no places to stand outside near the railing. So we found places inside the car and held onto the overhead straps. We didn't mind, since it was chilly outside, and at least we were onboard. We were a little cramped and had trouble seeing outside. But it was safe and warm and okay. *Okay*, however, wasn't part of my cable car fantasy.

Then it happened, just like in a movie. Two people who had been perched on the railing of the cable car stepped off, and Sandy said to me: "Let's get those spots and see what it's like riding out there." We raced over and stood side by side, hanging onto two poles at the edge of the car. We spent the next hour riding on the outside, and it was incredible.

We couldn't believe the difference between riding inside and outside. Standing by the railing with the brisk wind swirling around us, Sandy and I felt the pulse of the city. We felt alive and invigorated. We saw everything clearly. We heard all the sounds. We smelled all the scents. We called to people walking on the sidewalks and riding in their cars. We whizzed by pedestrians, cars, shops, and restaurants, with our feet just inches from the sidewalks. We laughed. We kissed. We had a blast.

That experience was an ideal metaphor for the difference between having an average, ordinary marriage and having a marriage based on spiritual intimacy. An average marriage is like riding *inside* the cable car. It may be safe and warm—it may be *okay*—but it's also boring. You have no idea what you're missing. When you spiritually bond, you move to the outside of the cable car. It's exhilarating. It's adventuresome. It's a rush. It's passionate. It's the ride of your lives.

## THE BEST KIND OF INTIMACY

Spiritual bonding creates genuine intimacy—the best and deepest kind. Coming together as a couple spiritually produces passion and energy unmatched in all of human experience. Nothing else can come close to matching it.

I'd like to conduct a little experiment. (We psychologists love experiments, so humor me.) I want you to recall the most intense and passionate physical time you've ever had with your spouse. Go ahead; picture it in your mind. Perhaps you were intoxicated by the sheer excitement and electricity of your lovemaking. Two bodies became one. Maybe it was during your honeymoon. Maybe it was ten years ago. Maybe it was last week.

Whatever magnificent physical interaction you're picturing pales in comparison to spiritual bonding. It's not even close. Sexual intercourse in marriage provides a great deal of pleasure and enjoyment. But even at its best, it can never reach the fulfillment and satisfaction brought by spiritual bonding.

Now I want you to picture the most vulnerable, open, and meaningful emotional time you've ever had with a member of the opposite sex. All the defenses were down. Nothing was in the way. You were talking on the deepest level possible. You were totally in tune with each other. You had never felt closer. Time stood still as your hearts entwined in love. Well, you get the idea.

For me, one of these deep emotional connections happened in 1981 in San Diego at a Bob's Big Boy restaurant. Since Bob's is a burger chain, it may sound like a strange place for a romantic interlude. But Sandy and I had been broken up for one year, and that evening at Bob's we got back together. I will never forget our five-hour conversation! We laughed and cried and poured out our hearts to each other. We talked about the previous year and the growth we had both experienced. We held hands, looked into each other's eyes, and agreed that our love would never die. The woman had finally come to her senses and realized that she was about to lose a major catch. Or was it me dropping to my knees, begging her to come back? I can't remember that part too well.

It was a life-changing conversation that led to our engagement and eventual marriage. Still, my experience at Bob's—and whatever emotional high you're picturing now—pale in comparison to spiritual bonding. There is simply no comparison. No matter how powerful it may be, no emotional high is even in the same league with a spiritual high.

## WORLD WAR II AND DALLAS SEMINARY

Have you ever seen a group of World War II veterans get together for a reunion? It's something to see! The instant recognition, the camaraderie, the hugs, the tears, and the stories of battles fought side by side all send one message to the observer: These men love each other and are bonded forever because they shared the experience of war. Fighting the enemy together forges a unique closeness that cannot be broken by time, geographical distance, or any other force.

Even though I've never been close to a world war, there was a time in my life when I faced intense, brutal pressure. It was the early 1980s, and I was a student at Dallas Theological Seminary. As a college graduate, I figured I wouldn't have a problem handling the academic requirements of the seminary. I was wrong—terribly wrong. I had never known such pressure, such a crushing workload, such demanding professors, and such incredibly unreasonable deadlines.

Now don't get me wrong. I loved Dallas Seminary, and I believe it is one of the finest theological institutions in the world.

But from day one, I felt as though I was fighting to keep my head above water. It was sink or swim. The name of the game for me and for my fellow soldiers in Stearns Hall, second floor, was *survival*. If you didn't find at least one guy to buddy up with, you sank without a trace.

My best war buddy at Dallas was Thom Provenzola. In that first year we lived just a few doors apart on the dorm floor. Together, we faced the never-ending assaults of our seminary professors, the avalanche of papers due every week, the thousands and thousands of pages of reading. And the tests—those impossibly long, diabolically complicated tests!

I will never forget (and believe me, I've tried) one particular class with one particular professor. Three times a week at the crack of dawn, Thom and I had to drag out of bed so we could get to this class by 7:00 A.M. Then we spent an hour and ten minutes feverishly taking notes from a man who spoke in the world's most boring monotone. Thom and I had to slap each other every ten minutes to keep from nodding off. I often wondered if the apostle Paul would have stayed awake in that class.

But the tests were the worst part of that class. We'd study our brains out for three or four days getting ready. Then at 7:00 A.M. on D day we'd file into class and be handed a test that would take any normal person three hours to complete. The only problem was that we had only an hour and ten minutes.

Thom and I would dig in and scribble our answers as fast as we possibly could. When the bell rang, we were totally and utterly drained. Our writing hands were frozen into claws. Our backs were sore. Our minds were mush. The final insult came when our professor handed back the graded tests. Every single time he told us—with a little smirk on his face—that his grader had trouble reading our writing. He would ask us, and I actually think he was serious, to please write more legibly next time. Thom and I wanted to scream, "Of course our tests have messy handwriting! Duh! You force us to complete a three-hour test in an hour and ten minutes!" But we said nothing to our professor. This was Dallas Seminary, and you don't do that there. We could only scream later when we were back in Stearns Hall.

In the pressure-packed, grueling crucible of Dallas Seminary, Thom and I forged a close friendship. It was us against the seminary, and we pulled each other through. We have never forgotten those days, and we remain the best of friends today.

Maybe you haven't been in a war or a grueling academic program, but I'll bet you've worked with someone toward a common goal—on a sports team, volunteer activity, a church committee, a class project, or the PTA at your child's school. If you have, then you know that working together brings you closer to that person.

Working together toward the greatest goal in life—knowing and loving God—creates the greatest closeness possible. Sandy and I have discovered this wonderful reality in our marriage. You and your partner can, too.

## LET THE WALLS FALL DOWN

When you connect spiritually in the presence of God, the walls between you and your partner come down. God tears them down. And when God tears walls down, they're down. You are two people, two souls, coming together to know God better, to worship Him, to love Him "with all your heart, and with all your soul, and with all your mind" (Matthew 22:37).

You'll still be a man and woman with differences and unique viewpoints. That doesn't change, and it shouldn't change. But you become male and female in the way God designed you to be. When you spiritually bond, your lives together become an adventurous, exhilarating ride—one characterized by unmatched closeness and intimacy.

# 6

# PHYSICAL LOVE
# AS YOU'VE NEVER
# KNOWN IT

~~∽᠙৽~~

### The Second Benefit: Great Sex

n my marriage enrichment seminars, I cite the Old Testament book Song of Solomon when I talk about physical intimacy. I always enjoy speaking on this text because it's such a beautiful, touching description of the glories of sex in a marriage relationship. I tell my audiences that God considers sex so important that He wrote a whole book about it.

Another reason I enjoy discussing the Song is the opportunity I get to talk to a crazy cast of characters after my presentation. It's amazing how people come out of the woodwork to give me a hard time about my interpretation of Solomon's book. Frankly, I find their comments entertaining.

Members of the "allegory gang," as I like to call them, always come up to set me straight. With their Bibles open and frowns on their faces, these extremely serious souls inform me that the Song of Solomon isn't about sex. It has nothing to do with sex. It's all an allegory, they assert. It's a picture of God's love for Israel, or of Christ's love for the Church. Anyone who interprets it as describing sex must have a dirty mind.

My typical response to the allegory gang is: "I'm sorry you are so uncomfortable with the topic of sex. God isn't uncomfortable with it at all. I've been to seminary, and I've studied the Song of Solomon carefully. I hate to be the one to tell you, but the book is, in fact, about sex."

Another group that disagrees with my view is the "sex whisperers." These folks pull me aside and say in hushed tones: "You shouldn't be talking about sex. And you certainly should never make it sound as though sex is for pleasure! Sex is a duty, a responsibility to your marriage partner. Its purposes are to meet a biological need and to have children. That's all."

It is true that the Bible teaches that sex should be actively engaged in as a duty, as a responsibility to the marriage partner (1 Corinthians 7:3, 5). But this aspect *alone* would not be sufficient motivation for the continual, regular sex life of a couple. Sex out of duty and responsibility alone would preclude tenderness and the expression of deep love on a continuing basis.

My response to the sex whisperers goes something like this: "That may be your opinion about sex, but it's not God's truth. The Song of Solomon is all about the pleasures of sex. Solomon and his bride, the Shulammite, are having loads of fun with sex all through the book. And God is thrilled by it. If your sex is boring and only a duty, you're missing God's best for you in this wonderful area. And that's a shame."

If sex is only what the sex whisperers think it is, God would not have provided us with an entire book describing in intimate detail the pleasures of sex and its profound benefits to the marriage relationship. He would not have designed us to be capable of the powerful, sensual, overwhelming experience of orgasm. He would not have created all those extremely sensitive areas of our bodies.

Also, if sex is only for making babies, wouldn't God have come up with some method other than the incredibly intimate and pleasurable one called intercourse? He could have made babies by the man simultaneously pinching the woman's nose while rubbing her kneecap. And sex only for procreation would most often mean having sex a handful of times in a lifetime, which would violate the clear teaching of Paul in 1 Corinthians. God gave us sex—this wonderful, fun, stress-relieving, unifying way to express love to each other.

At one seminar, a man actually came up to me and, with a straight face, told me that God was not in favor of all this intimate touching I was talking about. He proceeded to quote 1 Corinthians 7:1: "It is not good for a man to touch a woman." I couldn't help myself—I laughed out loud. Since the verse refers to *unmarried* people who, by engaging in sex, commit immorality, he was taking this verse wildly out of context. And I told him so. Then we had this little exchange:

> **Dave:** You're married, aren't you?
> **Man:** Yes, I am. (He introduced his wife. She did not look like a happy person.)
> **Dave:** Do you have children?
> **Man:** Yes. We have three.
> **Dave:** Well, please tell me how you got three kids without touching your wife! Unless they're all adopted, I'm betting you had to have intercourse at least three times.

I went on to tell this misguided man what Paul told the believers at Corinth:

> Let the husband fulfill his duty to his wife, and likewise also the wife to her husband. The wife does not have authority over her own body, but the husband does; and likewise also the husband does not have authority over his own body, but the wife does. Stop depriving one another, except by agreement for a time that you may devote yourselves to prayer, and come together

again lest Satan tempt you because of your lack of self-control. (1 Corinthians 7:3–5)

What God is saying here, I told this man, is that sexual intercourse is to be a regular practice between husband and wife. The only time it's okay to temporarily suspend intercourse is for the purpose of praying together (implying an interval set aside for intense prayer). This passage even warns them that if they *don't* have regular intercourse, they open the door to Satan's temptations.

As you might have guessed, I'm not the most diplomatic guy in the world. I have trouble with people who do not believe the clear teaching of the Bible. I try not to be too hard on these anti-Song of Solomon folks. They're not malicious. They just don't understand. I want you to understand, and I believe God wants you to understand.

God wants you and your spouse, as a married couple, to have a tremendous sex life—a passionate and meaningful physical union that is the very symbol of the *one-flesh* relationship. In chapter 2, I argued that sex by itself cannot be the basis for a close, lasting relationship (of course, the operative words are *by itself*). However, when you and your partner achieve spiritual intimacy, your sex life will become far more fulfilling than you ever thought possible.

## It All Starts with Two Bodies

Most normal, red-blooded people realize that physical love—physical passion—is a vital part of a relationship. Sexual touching is one of the most enjoyable activities in marriage. Who wants to be in a marriage relationship that has no physical intimacy? No touching? No kissing? No caressing? No intercourse? Nobody does. Husbands and wives are designed by God to need sexual touch.

Everyone is first attracted to a member of the opposite sex by that person's body. Of course, most people don't walk up to someone and say, "Hey, I was standing over there, and I couldn't help but notice you. I've got to tell you, I really like your body." Anyone who said that would probably never get any dates—and might get a slap in the face. But those thoughts certainly exist, and it's okay. It's how God made us.

When I saw Sandy for the first time, in front of the gym on the campus of Point Loma College, I didn't think, *Wow! What a great mind!* I hadn't even met her yet. I thought, *Whoa! She's beautiful!* And, of course, she was thinking the same thing about me. Well, her physical attraction to me wasn't quite as dramatic as the other way around. But she did think I was cute...in a Humphrey Bogart kind of way.

Physical chemistry between two persons happens immediately. It's just there. You either have it or you don't. Chances are, you and your spouse felt a physical attraction for each other when you first met. That's the ember of sexual desire that grows into a roaring blaze when you're married and experiencing spiritual intimacy.

Take a look at Solomon and the Shulammite woman in the Song of Solomon. The hormones leap off the pages! There's no way you can miss their immediate and powerful physical attraction to each other. It was intense. These lovers obviously had what I call the *"whoa."* The *whoa* is when you look at someone and can't help but say, "Whoa!" It's that physical spark between two people. It was pleasing to God for Solomon and his lover to feel this way. It was, in fact, just the way God planned it to be. These two famous biblical lovers are our examples. Physical attraction isn't everything in a relationship, but you've got to have it.

## THE SOURCE OF LASTING SEXUAL PASSION

God intended for husbands and wives to be physically attracted to each other and to experience sexual chemistry when they're together. He also intended a couple's spiritual relationship to energize their physical relationship.

It's been my experience, both personally and professionally, that there's something about spiritual bonding that enlivens a ho-hum sex life. Many couples whose sexual relationships are dull, stale, and routine come to me for sex therapy. What I give them is spiritual bonding therapy. It's certainly not what they expect, but it works.

I teach a variety of sexual techniques, and they do help. But the wellspring of sexual passion isn't found in any technique. It's found in spiritual closeness. What good are techniques when you have no desire, no passion? Every couple I've seen who has spiritually bonded reports a significant improvement in the sexual area.

Song of Solomon clearly shows God's idea of marital sex. In it, we read a beautiful description of sexual intercourse between Solomon and his bride on their wedding night:

> I have come into my garden, my sister, my bride; I have gathered my myrrh along with my balsam. I have eaten my honeycomb and my honey; I have drunk my wine and my milk. Eat, friends; drink and imbibe deeply, O lovers. (Song of Solomon 5:1)

Do you know who says this? It's God Himself! God is present with Solomon and the Shulammite in their wedding chamber. He is enjoying their physical intimacy. He is approving of it. He is blessing it. And, I believe, He is empowering it. God is the source of their sexual passion—on their wedding night and throughout their marriage.

Stay intimate with God as a couple, and you'll stay intimate sexually with each other. God wants you to experience the greatest sex possible—the kind of sex Solomon and the Shulammite had. If you bond spiritually, you can have this kind of sex for all the years of your marriage.

# 7

# WHATEVER HAPPENED TO CONVERSATION?

*The Third Benefit: Deep, Personal Communication*

One day, I had just finished lunch at home and was driving back to the office. It had been a particularly difficult couple of weeks in my therapy practice. I had seen a succession of married couples who didn't talk to each other. Their communication was just about nonexistent. Except for "good morning" and "pass the potatoes," these couples didn't have anything to say to each other. I was beginning to wonder if there was even one married couple in Tampa Bay with a halfway decent level of communication.

Then it happened. As I drove down a quiet residential street near my home, I noticed a man and a woman walking together on the sidewalk. I felt a burst of hope and thought, *Well, it's about time I came across a couple who actually enjoys being together. Look at that sweet picture. A husband and his dear wife, spending quality time talking as they get a little exercise. They're not holding hands, but you can't have everything. At least they're communicating. Maybe there's hope for marriages after all.*

My warm, wistful bubble exploded as I drove close enough

to see what was really going on. I observed, with horror, that they each were wearing a Walkman! They weren't talking at all! They weren't even looking at each other. They were bebopping along to music emanating from the cassette players hanging on their belts.

I lost control. I snapped. I pulled alongside the couple, rolled down my window, and shouted: "What's the matter with you two? You are wasting a golden opportunity to build your marriage! Why are you listening to music and not talking to each other? Why do you even bother walking together at all? What are you, a couple of zombies? You ought to be ashamed of yourselves!"

Okay, I didn't say those things to this couple. They wouldn't have been able to hear me if I had. Oh, I wanted to. But the man was about six feet two, two hundred fifty pounds, and I would have hated to pin him to the ground in front of his wife. Instead, I muttered my comments to myself in the privacy and safety of my car.

This walking-but-not-talking couple is an all too accurate snapshot of the state of conversation in most marriages. So many husbands and wives don't talk to each other in a deep, revealing, and meaningful way. They don't connect. They live separate lives. They don't truly know each other. They don't know how to communicate. They don't know how to overcome the many obstacles between them and great dialogue.

## "He Won't Talk to Me!"

I've talked to thousands of women in my office and at my seminars. Over the years, I've received hundreds of letters, e-mails, and phone calls from women. I've heard every possible complaint about husbands. Of course, I've also heard Sandy's complaints about me—many times. The number one complaint of women of all ages can be summed up in five words: "He won't talk to me!" I use an exclamation point because this lack of communication really, really bothers women.

Every woman's most cherished desire is that her husband will open up and share his innermost self with her. He's a good guy. She knows he loves her. He's a good provider. He's a good dad. He has integrity, and she can trust him. She loves him for all these qualities. But she wants more. She longs to know him—to know what he's thinking and feeling. She has a powerful need to be emotionally close to him—to be not just his mate, but also his soul mate.

She realizes that the only way to experience emotional closeness is through conversation. So she tries all kinds of methods and approaches to motivate him to talk on a deeper level. But no matter how hard she tries, he refuses to open up. She's sweet and loving—he clams up. She begs—he clams up. She cries—he clams up. She gets angry and intense—he clams up. She fills the air with words, hoping that something she says will trigger a response—he clams up. Nothing works.

Most men, by nature, conceal and hold in their thoughts and feelings. When their wives probe to get at what's inside, men automatically respond by shutting down. They feel pressured and will not talk about their inner life.

## "I DON'T KNOW WHAT SHE WANTS!"

Although men put up many barriers to emotional closeness, women are just as guilty of preventing conversational intimacy. I've also talked to thousands of men and heard all their complaints about their wives. One of their biggest beefs is the way wives talk in code. Women use a special language to communicate their needs to their husbands. Unfortunately, men have no idea how to crack this code.

The woman will tell the man what she wants him to do. At least, she thinks that she has told him. She actually believes that she sent a crystal-clear message, which only an insensitive, uncaring lout could miss. The man does miss it, because she sent the message in her female code. When he fails to meet her need, she's upset. It's his fault! He's selfish! He's in trouble, and he doesn't even know why.

Suppose a wife gets off the phone and says to her husband, "That was my friend Susie. I haven't talked to her for a while. She's going to a craft class this Saturday morning. I'll bet that's going to be fun. I used to do crafts all the time." She *thinks* she said, "Susie's going to the craft class, and I want to go with her. I miss her and want to renew our friendship. Even though I enjoy crafts, it's not really about crafts. It's about our relationship. She's reaching out to me, and that feels good. Is it okay with you if I go?"

Another woman would have immediately gotten Susie's real, underlying message. Unfortunately, this wife is married to a man, and he didn't get the message because she never sent it, at least not in language he could understand.

Come Saturday morning, she's an emotional wreck because she has been waiting for him to encourage her to go to the craft class with her friend. He has no idea what's going on. He's completely forgotten about the class! It's going to be an ugly scene when she pours out her pain to him.

She thinks he realizes that she wants to go to the craft class so she can spend time with her friend. She goes into a twenty-minute monologue about how little time she has for friends. One time—one lousy time—she has a chance to be with a friend, and he denies it to her. Her assumption that he got her message is incorrect! She has *created* this imaginary scenario about her husband's insensitivity and injustice.

Is this fair? No! Is it the way most wives operate? You better believe it. The woman incorrectly assumes that she is sending a clear message to her husband. When he does nothing, her fury builds and builds because she concludes that he's a thoughtless, heartless nincompoop.

## How Do We Connect in Conversation?

Both men and women are guilty of killing conversation and with it, emotional intimacy (which, of course, leads to physical intimacy). There are many barriers to true emotional closeness, and without good communication and the intimate connections it creates, you can't have much of a marriage. A great marriage is a series of great conversations.

It is, in fact, critical to connect in conversation and produce an ongoing, vibrant emotional bond. You need to understand basic male-female differences, share openly and honestly, and learn to communicate on a deeper level. I teach seminars on these topics. I wrote a book on communication skills in marriage (*Men Are Clams, Women Are Crowbars*).

Although communication techniques do help in the creation of emotional intimacy, they are not enough on their own. How many times have you and your spouse gone to a seminar, read a book, or watched a video and experienced only a brief burst of improvement? After just a few weeks or months, you slipped back into your old intimacy-killing patterns.

Well, what's the answer? How can we break through all these barriers to intimacy and achieve long-term marital joy and fulfillment? Here's the answer: *Both physical and emotional intimacy are essential, and there are specific things you can do as a couple to improve them. But the main, continuing source of both physical and emotional intimacy is spiritual bonding.* Not many people know this. And the price for not knowing it is the absence of great conversations. With a deep spiritual bond, a husband can stop clamming up and share with his wife what's inside. With a deep spiritual bond, a wife can stop talking in code and clearly communicate her personal needs to her husband.

Both of these barriers to emotional intimacy stem from insecurity and fear. The man doesn't want to appear vulnerable, lest he be seen as inadequate or weak. He's scared of losing control. He feels safe hiding behind his strong, silent image. The woman isn't sure the man loves her for the right reasons. Does he love her for what she does for him (sex, chores, child care), or for who she is? It's safer to test him with unclear language than to come right out in the open with her needs and deep feelings.

Spiritual bonding provides the confidence to be open, vulnerable, and direct with your spouse. It gives you both the confidence that Christ alone can give. Spiritual bonding also connects you on a deeper level. When you bond in spiritual intimacy, you are automatically in touch spiritually. This spiritual closeness flows into emotional closeness. When you bond spiritually, you gradually and more deeply reveal who you really are. Consider these powerful words about love: "Its flashes are flashes of fire, the very flame of the Lord" (Song of Solomon 8:6). God is the only source of genuine love. Is your love the "flame of the Lord"? If you want this kind of love—and I know you do—you have to spiritually bond.

# STAY OUT OF THE
# MARRIAGE GRAVEYARD

*The Fourth Benefit: Protection from Relationship Killers*

'm going to take you on a brief tour of a marriage graveyard. In it are buried all the marriages whose deaths I've personally witnessed. Some are marriages I've worked with as a therapist. Some I've had contact with through my seminars. Still others, the most painful of all, are the marriages of friends and family members. It's a sad place, but a place where valuable lessons can be learned.

I walk through this graveyard from time to time to remind myself of the many ways a marriage can be killed. All the couples whose marriages are buried here loved each other at one time. Many of them knew Christ and believed that they had a Christian marriage. They planned to live together for life. Not one of these couples thought that their marriage would end in this horrible place, six feet under.

No marriage dies of natural causes. It has to be killed by the behavior of one or both spouses. My marriage, and your marriage, could easily be killed if we make the same mistakes these couples made. Come with me now as I read the cause of death written on the headstones of these marriages.

## Killed by Work

Here lies a marriage murdered by the husband's workaholism. He wanted to succeed in business so badly that he made his job his top priority. He'd leave early in the morning and get home late in the evening. He brought work home and often worked on the weekends. He told his wife, "I'm working for you and the kids." He promised to spend more time with the family; he said he'd be home more "when things lighten up." But things never did lighten up. He succeeded in business, but the price was a dead marriage and a couple of heartbroken kids.

## Killed by Children

She'd always dreamed of being a mom. When she had her three children, she threw herself into their lives. She was going to be the best mom ever. She did everything for her kids: bathed them, clothed them, played with them, read to them, prayed with them, talked with them, did homework with them, cooked and cleaned for them. Along the way, she forgot that she was a wife, too. She neglected her husband for years. Her duties as a mom always seemed to get in the way of being a lover, a friend, and a partner to her husband. She's still a mom, but now she sleeps alone.

## Killed by Alcohol

He enjoyed a few beers after work and on the weekends. He said drinking helped him relax and unwind. How could anybody watch a ball game without cracking open a cold one? It was no big deal, he said. He wasn't hurting anybody. He didn't have a problem. What he did have was a big, fat case of denial. It wasn't just a few beers. It was eight, nine, or ten beers in one sitting. It was whiskey and vodka. It was stupid jokes, vicious rages, and falling asleep night after night in his chair. It was arguments with his wife. It was little time with his kids. It was, after twelve years, the end of his marriage.

## KILLED BY PRESCRIPTION DRUGS

She started taking painkillers after an operation. She was supposed to fill only one prescription and be off the pills in three weeks. But she had stress in her life, and the pills made her feel good. She got hooked. She invented all kinds of aches and pains and saw doctors all over town. She built a huge supply of pills and hid them around the house. Slowly but surely, she withdrew from her husband and kids. She had rages, violent mood swings, and days when she would shut herself in her room. She's still taking the pills, but she doesn't have to worry about spending time with her husband and children. She's divorced and sees the kids only in supervised visitation every other weekend.

## KILLED BY TELEVISION AND COMPUTER

He was a television junkie. He just couldn't get enough TV. He'd turn on the set as soon as he got home from work and leave it on until he went to bed. It was company. It was entertainment. He said that it helped him deal with his stressful job. With a hundred and fifty channels, he could always find something to watch. The only thing that finally pried him away from his television set was his new computer. He loved checking his e-mail, playing games, and surfing the Internet. For years, he spent night after night either watching TV or glued to his computer monitor. His wife died a thousand deaths waiting for him to give her some time and attention. She got tired of waiting. Now he has all the time in the world to play with his computer and watch television without the distraction of a wife and children.

## COUNTERFEITS OF INTIMACY

As I turn to leave the graveyard, I look over the rows and rows of tombstones. It strikes me that all the specific behaviors listed as causes of death have one thing in common: They are counterfeits of intimacy. They are behaviors outside the marriage relationship that promise fulfillment and passion, but end up destroying us and our marriages.

Every person—and I mean *every* person—has at least one counterfeit of intimacy. It is an area of weakness that you are drawn to. It's always around. It's right outside the door of your life, waiting. But it doesn't wait passively. It calls to you, promising fun and excitement and, yes, even intimacy.

In the New Testament, James does not mince words about the insidious process of sin:

> Each one is tempted when, by his own evil desire, he is dragged away and enticed. Then, after desire has conceived, it gives birth to sin; and sin, when it is full-grown, gives birth to death. (James 1:14–15, NIV)

Sounds familiar, doesn't it? How many times have you seen people you know ruin their lives by chasing after some sinful behavior? Maybe it's happened to you. Maybe it's happening right now in your life.

Our counterfeits cannot deliver anything healthy. They certainly cannot deliver intimacy in any way, shape, or form. They can only lead to death. If you play with your counterfeit, it will end up killing you, your marriage, and your family.

My counterfeit of intimacy is work. God has gifted me to do what I do, and I love all the aspects of my job. I love doing therapy with individuals, couples, and families. I love speaking. I love teaching seminary classes. I love writing books. I love doing radio shows about marriage and family issues.

I love what I do so much that I can get carried away. There are times when I become overcommitted, and my schedule gets too full. I begin to look to my career to meet my needs for attention, importance, and emotional fulfillment. Without realizing it, I neglect my wife and children.

Fortunately, it usually doesn't take me long to recognize that I'm swilling at the trough of my counterfeit. I have two people who are not afraid to get me back on track. My wife and my great friend Rocky Glisson are always there to hit me upside the head with the truth. Sandy will say, in her kind and gentle way, "Hey, Mr. Big Shot Psychologist! Remember me and the four children you've given me? We need you at home." Rocky will look at me sharply and say, "David, you're an idiot. You teach others that family is a priority. Live it."

So, what's your counterfeit? Is it work, children, alcohol, drugs, television, or the computer? Maybe it's an area I haven't mentioned yet. Check out this list and see if you recognize anything:

- sports
- church involvement
- entertainment
- hobbies/crafts
- food
- gambling
- cigarettes
- pets
- shopping
- exercise
- money
- power
- fame
- SEX

## THE POWER OF LUST

That last one on the list jumps out at me—and not just because I put it all in capital letters. Sex has literally exploded as a destructive force in society. Over the past ten years, I've watched sexual lust wipe out marriage after marriage. "Killed by Lust" is the epitaph etched in grim finality on millions of marriage tombstones. If sex isn't the number one counterfeit of intimacy, for both men and women, it's awfully close.

In our rapidly deteriorating Western culture, sex has become a counterfeit of epidemic proportions. As I said in chapter 2, sex is everywhere, promising easy stimulation, passion, and escape. Oh, it can deliver these things temporarily. And when you're hooked, you'll spend more and more time and energy looking for your next fix.

A startling picture of just how completely lust can take over a life can be found in experimental laboratories at major universities across the world. In these laboratories, behavioral psychologists perform a variety of tests on rats. As a general rule, I'm not too impressed with rat experiments. As a psychologist, I work with human beings, and human beings—most of them anyway—are much different from rats. Nevertheless, some fascinating experiments have been done with rats that reveal the power of sex.

Typically, a rat is placed in a cage. Inside the cage, on one side near the floor, there is a small lever. The rat bangs around the cage for several minutes, sniffing and exploring. When, quite by accident, the rat hits the lever, he receives a reward. In such experiments, usually it's a pellet of food or a drink of water. In one study, however, the rat received a sexual stimulation when the lever was hit. This rat had electrodes implanted in a particular part of his brain, and when he hit the lever, he experienced a rat orgasm.

In study after study replicating this experiment, the same startling results have been produced. After the first stimulation, the rat hits the lever, and hits the lever, and hits the lever. Scores of times, hundreds of times, the rat hits that lever and gets the stimulation until, finally, he dies. I'm serious! The rat stops giving himself orgasms only when he's taken out of the cage in a rat body bag.

It's sad to say, but humans seem to be just as prone as rats to sex addiction. Just like rats, humans have sexual pleasure centers in their brains. Just like rats, humans can give up everything in a headlong rush to satisfy their sexual needs. I've seen hundreds of men and women allow lust to destroy their lives and marriages.

I've highlighted sex because it's such a widespread and lethal counterfeit. Be careful, though, not to breathe a sigh of relief if sex isn't your particular counterfeit. Whatever your area of weakness, it has the power to crush you and everyone you hold dear.

## SATAN AT HIS BEST—OR WORST

You may be the only *person* who knows what your counterfeit is. But please don't think for a moment that it's a secret. God knows. And a certain someone else knows. That someone is Satan. He knows your name, he knows where you live, he knows your spouse, and he knows your kids. He spends all his time trying to drag you down.

Satan is incredibly evil. He is also incredibly powerful. He is the "prince of this world." He hates your guts and will do everything he can in his awesome might and craftiness to destroy you and your marriage. His favorite tool of destruction is your counterfeit of intimacy.

Do you think it's a coincidence that when you and your spouse are at a low point, you just happen to meet an attractive member of the opposite sex? Someone who is attentive, a great listener, and so caring? It's no coincidence. It's Satan and his marriage-breaking dating service! He waits for the opportunity to tempt you to immorality (see 1 Corinthians 7:5).

Whatever your counterfeit is, Satan will put it right in front of you at just the right time: when you're stressed, when you're tired, when you're lonely, when you've been traumatized, when you're depressed, when you're anxious, when you need an ego boost. You can bet Satan never misses an opportunity to go for your jugular.

## Intimacy or Disaster?

I hope I've alarmed you. The stakes are extremely high, and you and I are walking a thin line between marital intimacy and marital disaster. The question is, how can we avoid our counterfeits of intimacy and get our needs met in the right places—especially when Satan is cramming our counterfeits down our throats every chance he gets?

There is a way—spiritual bonding. This is not the only weapon we have in our battle against Satan and our counterfeits, but it is one of the most effective. Our weapons are not "of the flesh, but divinely powerful" (2 Corinthians 10:4). Satan can't stand up to spiritual power. When we are bonded spiritually to each other and to Jesus Christ, we have God's power on our side. And that's more than enough.

If you are not spiritually bonded to your partner, you will not experience true intimacy. As a result, you will be drawn to your counterfeit of intimacy. If you don't have God at the center of your life and your relationship, something else will be at the center. And we both know what that something else will be, don't we?

If you don't "hunger and thirst for righteousness" (Matthew 5:6), you'll still be hungry and thirsty. Picture yourself standing in front of a cool, fresh pool of water literally dying of thirst. It's just a matter of time before you drink! The pool is your counterfeit of intimacy. Oh, you can hold out for a while through sheer will power. But eventually, you'll drink. You'll guzzle. You'll dive in.

If, however, you have quenched—and are quenching—your thirst from another pool, you can stand before the counterfeit pool and not drink. You'll be satisfied, filled up. The pool you need to drink from is spiritual bonding.

When you spiritually bond with your partner, you will experience the true intimacy that God designed you to enjoy. You will connect on a deep level with Jesus Christ and your mate, and your most important needs will be met. Your pool of counterfeit intimacy will always be there. You have to walk by it every day of your life. Satan makes sure of that. But with your thirst for real intimacy satisfied through this spiritual bond, you can walk by it and not drink.

Every marriage goes through tough times—times when life is painful, times when your physical and emotional intimacy seem to be all dried up. There will be moments when you doubt that you're in love anymore. You'll wonder if you really want to spend the rest of your life with this person.

In these dry, difficult times, the only thing that will keep your marriage alive is a spiritual connection. Both of you will be seriously tempted to return to your counterfeit. Maybe one of you has already gone to a counterfeit, and the marriage has been damaged. Satan will see his chance to kill your love, and he'll go for it. Spiritual bonding will help you escape disaster and help you hang onto your relationship long enough to heal and rebuild. As the apostle Paul tells us:

> No temptation has overtaken you but such as is common to man; and God is faithful, who will not allow you to be tempted beyond what you are able, but with the temptation will provide the way of escape also, that you may be able to endure it. (1 Corinthians 10:13)

Through every kind of temptation, when Satan seeks to destroy your marriage, a strong spiritual bond will hold you and your spouse together.

# 9

# DON'T LET YOUR MARRIAGE RUN OUT OF GAS

*The Fifth Benefit: Fuel to Go the Distance*

t sixteen, I got my first car—a bright yellow '69 Camaro with white upholstery, bucket seats, and a stick shift. I loved that car. Two years later, just before I left for college, my dad gave me his flashy, red Pontiac Firebird. It was a real step up. That car was sleek, powerful, and fast.

Unfortunately, after sitting near the ocean in San Diego for a year, my Firebird had huge rust spots all over it. It was time to get another car, and I had high hopes. I figured my third car would be another sports car, an even flashier one. I thought my dad would give me his car: a beautiful, unbelievably cool Datsun 280Z. What a car! It was as close to a racecar as I was ever going to get. In my goggles and bright red scarf, I would own the road in that Z.

My dad didn't need that car. After all, he was in his forties, and life had passed him by. He didn't need to impress the ladies. He was an old married man. I needed a babe-magnet car, and that Z filled the bill. I could just see myself cruising the campus at Point Loma College in my Z, followed by a huge crowd of lovely college women. And I envisioned the conversations I would have:

"Wow, Dave, you look so cool in that car! Can I have a ride?"

"Why, sure, Bambi. Hop in."

You can see that, at eighteen, I had my priorities in order.

But alas, my dream did not come true. My fast-car fantasy hit a huge speed bump. My dad wouldn't let me *drive* his car, much less own it.

So I ended up with…a Toyota Corona station wagon.

It was like going from a possible stay in the presidential suite at the Ritz Carlton to a room by the ice machine in a Motel 6. I'm not sure, but I think my dad may have been punishing me for letting his Firebird rust out.

My station wagon wouldn't attract women—it would repel them. I wouldn't get their attention—I'd get their pity. I mean, an eighty-five-year-old man wouldn't be caught dead in a Corona. Of course, I didn't say those things to my dad. What could I say? He didn't lose sleep worrying about my social life. Plus, he was paying for the car, not to mention my college tuition.

Actually, in time I grew fond of my little Corona wagon. It was dependable. It got great gas mileage. It was, in its own way, kind of cute. I consoled myself with the knowledge that women would go out with me just for *me,* not my car.

But there was one major problem with my Corona. It ran out of gas. Frequently. Soon after I drove it from Florida to California, the gas gauge broke. After I filled the tank, the needle would just barely nudge above empty. I never knew just how much gas I had in that car. Even worse, I was a poor college student, and I could put only three or four dollars worth of gas in at a time.

I ran out of gas in that crazy car over and over again. I must have run out of gas ten or twelve times that first year. I'd be sailing along, sure that I had plenty of gas. Then the engine would cough a few times, sputter, and die. I would scream, "No! Not again!" And I'd coast to a stop on the side of the road. I'd get out, trudge to the nearest gas station, fill up a small gas container, and trudge back to the Corona.

Once I ran out of gas with Sandy in the car. We'd been dating for only a few months, and we were planning to go to the movies and then park in a romantic spot. (Okay, the parking part was my idea.) We ended up parking a lot sooner than I'd anticipated because the Corona coasted to a stop just a few miles from the Point Loma campus. Sandy wasn't impressed. She thought I'd done it on purpose!

Here's the point of my story: Your marriage is a lot like my little Corona station wagon. It may run out of gas before you complete the marriage journey. You and your spouse might run beautifully for a while on your first tank of chemistry, passion, and sexual attraction. But chances are that it won't last. Just like my Corona, your tank will unexpectedly go dry, and you'll coast to a stop by the side of the road. There are millions of stalled marriages on the highway of life. What we need is a reservoir of fuel so we can go the distance.

## MAKE SURE THE TANK IS FULL

Why do marriages run out of gas? Continuing my car analogy (because I like it), keep picturing your marriage as a car. The body is your physical relationship; the engine is your emotional relationship. Now, the body and the engine are obviously key parts of the car. You can't do without them. But what makes the car run? The fuel, of course. And *spiritual bonding* is the fuel—the only fuel—that makes a love relationship run, move, and operate.

Would God make us spiritual beings and then allow us to have complete satisfaction and intimacy by ignoring the spiritual part of marriage? No. God has designed man-woman relationships in such a way that they will not work without Him at the center.

Referring to Christ, the apostle Paul said, "And He is before all things, and in Him all things hold together" (Colossians 1:17). And in John 15:5, Jesus Himself says: "I am the vine, you are the branches; he who abides in Me, and I in him, he bears much fruit; for apart from Me you can do nothing." Even though these verses are not referring directly to marriage, I believe the message applies. When Christ is not at the center of your personal life, it is a disaster. When Christ is not at the center of your relationship, it is a disaster. In time, things fall apart, and you lose everything.

Does it make sense that if you put God at the center of your marriage, He will bless every other area? That's exactly what He'll do! What happens when you put God, Jesus Christ, and the Holy Spirit at the center of your personal life? You reap the fruit of the Spirit: love, joy, peace, patience, kindness, goodness, faithfulness, gentleness, and self-control (see Galatians 5:22–23). These same benefits come when you, as a couple, put God at the center of your marriage. Would you like the fruit of the Spirit in your marriage? With a strong spiritual bond, you can have it.

## A Truly Christian Marriage

On a regular basis, I ask churchgoing couples this simple question: "Do you have a Christian marriage?" Here are the most common responses:

- Yes, we're both Christians.
- We pray before meals.
- We attend church.
- We're involved in the church.
- We believe the same doctrine.
- We both have regular quiet times with God.
- We both love Jesus Christ.

Then I tell these couples: "These things, even if you add them all together, do not give you a Christian marriage. At best, you individually have a healthy, growing relationship with Jesus

Christ. That's great! Keep it up! But you are on separate, parallel tracks. You're both going in the same direction, but you're getting there on your own."

In a truly Christian marriage, your two parallel tracks regularly intersect and become one. You still grow spiritually as individuals, but you also grow spiritually as a couple. Read these verses and ask yourself if they describe your marriage:

> So that Christ may dwell in your hearts through faith; and that you, being rooted and grounded in love, may be able to comprehend with all the saints what is the breadth and length and height and depth, and to know the love of Christ which surpasses knowledge, that you may be filled up to all the fullness of God. (Ephesians 3:17–19)

Paul isn't talking specifically to married people here, but I am convinced that every married couple can experience this kind of love in Christ by spiritually bonding. If God wants you to comprehend the matchless love of Christ "with all the saints," He certainly wants you to comprehend it with your spouse.

Truly Christian marriages aren't born—they're made. Most couples don't have Christian marriages for two reasons. First, they don't realize the importance of spiritual bonding. (After reading this far, I hope you do realize its importance.) Second, they just don't know *how* to spiritually bond.

You want all the benefits of spiritual intimacy I've described, don't you? I know you're eager to find out how to spiritually bond. Beginning with the next chapter, I'm going to show you how.

 OW TO

 PIRITUALLY

 OND WITH

OUR POUSE

# 10

# THE GREATEST
# ADVENTURE

*The Thrill of Ongoing Spiritual Growth*

f you want to see one of the greatest adventure movies ever made, go to your local video store and rent Alfred Hitchcock's *North by Northwest*. What a movie! Its nonstop action and wild twists and turns will keep your heart pounding and your bottom on the edge of your seat. Cary Grant plays a New York advertising executive who is forced into a deadly game of cat and mouse with a criminal mastermind played by James Mason. Mason thinks Grant is a CIA agent working to break up his spy ring, and he spends the entire movie trying to kill him. Grant has no idea what's going on, and he spends the entire movie trying to stay alive and figure out what Mason is up to.

Mason and his minions send Grant careening down a mountain in his car. They frame him for a very public murder at the United Nations. In one thrilling scene in a cornfield, they send a crop duster to machine-gun him to death. The resourceful Grant barely manages to escape all these harrowing experiences and continues to doggedly pursue the evil Mason.

If all this action weren't enough, there's also a sizzling

romance between Grant and the lovely Eva Marie Saint. Eva is, like most women, alluring but incredibly complicated. She saves Cary from being captured by the police, and they fall in love. Then Cary finds out that she's Mason's mistress, and he hates her guts. Then he finds out that she's a CIA agent who has infiltrated Mason's organization, and he falls in love with her again. In the final, climactic scene, Cary and Eva wage a desperate hand-to-hand battle with Mason's henchmen on the faces of Mount Rushmore. Cary saves Eva's life, and they get married and live happily ever after.

Even though *North by Northwest* is just a movie, I firmly believe that a spiritually intimate couple can experience a life together that is just as adventurous as Cary and Eva's—though hopefully not as dangerous and perilous! You and your spouse won't be battling an evil mastermind every time you turn around. You won't be fighting for your lives on Mount Rushmore. No one wants that kind of adventure! But in the journey of spiritual bonding, you will face together a never-ending series of exciting, unpredictable twists and turns that enrich your personal lives and marriage.

It is God's desire and plan that your marriage be the greatest adventure you could ever experience. Like a superbly skilled movie director, God Himself will orchestrate every frame, every step of your real-life drama. He'll bring events into your lives that will strengthen your bond to Him and to each other. He'll create circumstances that will bring you closer and closer in your love. What could be more exciting than walking with God every day as a couple and seeing His hand in all you do?

To live the adventure of spiritual bonding, a couple must meet two critical prerequisites. First, each person in the relationship must be a Christian. To spiritually bond, both partners must be *spiritually alive*. Second, each person in the relationship must be *growing* in Christ. When you are both growing spiritually, you can share that growth and become more intimate in Christ.

## ONLY ONE WAY TO GOD

There is a lot of confusion these days about what makes someone a Christian. Millions of people call themselves Christians and believe that they will go to heaven when they die. But when pressed for specifics about their faith, they can't articulate what it is that makes them a Christian.

There is, in fact, only one way to reach the true God, and that is through His Son, Jesus Christ. In John 14:6, the writer records these words of Jesus: "I am the way, and the truth, and the life; no one comes to the Father, but through Me." When you believe that Jesus died on the cross for all your sins, that He was resurrected, and that His shed blood brings atonement for your sins, you are a Christian. You have been "made alive in Christ." You are spiritually alive.

The second step toward developing spiritual intimacy—each spouse maturing in his or her walk with Christ—energizes your growth as a couple. Read the following verses and think about your personal relationship with Jesus:

What does the LORD your God require from you, but to fear the LORD your God, to walk in all His ways and love Him, and to serve the LORD your God with all your heart and with all your soul? (Deuteronomy 10:12)

Grace to all who love our Lord Jesus Christ with an undying love. (Ephesians 6:24, NIV)

I count all things to be loss in view of the surpassing value of knowing Christ Jesus my Lord, for whom I have suffered the loss of all things, and count them but rubbish in order that I may gain Christ. (Philippians 3:8)

Is your love for Christ this deep, this committed, this passionate? If not, Christ's words in Revelation 2:4 may be true of you: "But I have this against you, that you have left your first love." Go back to your first love. Jesus is waiting patiently for you to spend time with Him—to read His Word, to listen to Him, to serve Him. Your daily walk with Christ is not only crucial for your personal life, but it's also vital for spiritual bonding with your partner.

Part of the spiritual bond Sandy and I have comes from our private, personal relationship with God. On our own, we each actively pursue a closer and richer walk with Him. I have a daily quiet time in which I pray, read the Bible, meditate, and study a devotional. I talk to God throughout the day and serve Him as He brings opportunities my way. Sandy works on her own spiritual life in many of these same ways.

We spiritually bond when we come together on a regular basis and share the personal growth we are experiencing. I tell Sandy the insights I've gained from my Bible reading, how God is working in my life, and what I believe God wants me to learn during the next several months. Sandy then tells me what's going on in her spiritual life. This is deep, honest sharing, and it creates a powerful bond between us.

Sandy and I didn't always spiritually bond like we do now. It's humbling to admit, but for years *I* was the main stumbling block. We couldn't spiritually bond on a deep level because I wasn't growing spiritually. I loved the Lord, but I was not committed to getting to know Him better. My quiet times were infrequent and brief. My Bible reading was superficial. My prayer life was the same old ten-minute tape of confessed sins and requests. I prayed in a heartfelt, earnest way only when I was in trouble and needed help.

Looking back, my feeble walk with Jesus Christ was a result of a number of factors. I was far too focused on my career. I was just plain lazy. I was intimidated by Sandy's spirituality. I was scared of being the spiritual leader, so I remained a stalled Christian to keep from taking on that role. I also feared what God might ask me to do if I were closer to Him. Secretly, I didn't want to give control of my life to God.

Finally, after years of living a lukewarm Christian life, I rededicated my life to Christ. The first Promise Keepers event I attended shook me up and got me on the right spiritual track. I will never forget how Dr. Crawford Loritts moved me to tears during a Promise Keepers session at Tampa Stadium. My ongoing accountability relationship with my pal Rocky Glisson has helped me to continue maturing in Christ. (Besides, Rocky is a big guy, and he just might hurt me if I drifted from God.)

As I've grown spiritually, my marriage has blossomed. Seeking to be more like Christ has automatically made me a better husband. I've finally stepped up as the spiritual leader. Rather than being threatened by Sandy's strong spiritual life, I'm now genuinely interested in what's happening between Jesus and her. And when I get a spiritual insight or I see God moving in my life, Sandy is the first person I tell. We are sharing Christ these days, and He is blessing our marriage in too many ways to count.

If your marriage is like mine, you and your spouse will grow at different rates. That's okay. The important thing is that you're both growing. A big part of the spiritual bond I'm talking about is sharing the personal growth you each experience, but you can't share what you don't have.

# 11

# PRAYER PARTNERS

*The Heart of Spiritual Bonding*

everal years ago, I counseled a couple whose marriage was over. At least, they thought it was over. Years of neglect and unresolved conflict had sucked all the intimacy out of their relationship. Both of them were Christians who attended church regularly with their two children. But their faith was weak, and they believed that not even God could save their marriage.

Like many couples I've seen, they came in only so they could say that they had tried counseling and it didn't work. Then they could rationalize that divorce was their only option. In essence, my office was the last stop before the attorneys and the divorce court.

In that first session, they told me their sad story. The husband was a selfish workaholic who had ignored his wife and kids. He had stopped expressing love for her years ago. The only time he paid any attention to her at all was when he wanted sex.

The wife was a terrible housekeeper and spent too much money. She was a world-class nag and had carped at him about his shortcomings for years. A hard shell of critical indifference covered her desperate desire to be loved. Her life revolved around the kids, the PTA, and church activities. Her husband had deeply wounded her, and she couldn't see how she could possibly love him again.

They finished their prepared statements and waited patiently for me to speak. They wanted a doctor to declare that their marriage was dead, but they were disappointed. I told them what I tell every couple who comes to see me: "It's not over. It doesn't have to be over, no matter how bad things look and feel. With hard work and God's help, you can love each other again. In fact, you can build a new marriage that will be everything God intended it to be."

They didn't exactly jump up and shout: "Yeah! We can do it! Thanks for that shot in the arm!" They just sat there, staring at me in silence. Then they looked at each other, as if to say: "This guy just doesn't get it, does he?"

I ended the session by going over the step-by-step approach I planned to take in their marriage therapy. I asked them to spend the next week thinking, praying, and soul-searching about their marriage. They scheduled another appointment for the following week and then shuffled slowly out of my office. Their situation looked grim, I admit, and I prayed that God would perform a miracle.

The next week, I watched this same couple drive into my parking lot and stroll down the walkway to my office. I couldn't believe my eyes. They were holding hands, smiling, and laughing—just as couples do when they're in love. When they came into my office and sat down on the couch, I said: "I don't know who you two are, but what have you done with the Smiths?"

They looked at each other in a knowing way and then told me an incredible story. They said that they had gone home after the previous week's session ready to end their marriage. After three days of silence, the husband suddenly asked his wife to pray with him. He told her that he was desperate and that the only option left was to turn to God. And so they prayed. And prayed. And prayed.

For three solid hours, they cried out to God on their knees in their bedroom. They confessed their sins in the relationship and repented of the many things they had done to hurt each other. They admitted their resentments and gave them all to God. Through tears, they asked for forgiveness—from God and from each other.

They told me that something amazing happened after those three hours of prayer. Forgiveness and healing happened. They felt cleansed. They felt hopeful. They felt passion and love for each other for the first time in years. With God's help, they knew they really could start over.

To be sure, this couple still had hard work to do in therapy. We spent several months clearing away old debris and building a new marriage. But their prayer marathon was the beginning of their journey. They now had God's help to apply the relationship principles I taught them. They determined to continue praying together regularly. No doubt because of that commitment, they are still together and have a great marriage.

What happened to this couple was, indeed, a miracle. Their story illustrates the dramatic power of prayer. Prayer can provide the same miraculous intervention for you and your marriage partner, even though you may not be in a crisis situation. It will create wonderful results no matter what condition your marriage is in. Every time you pray as a couple, it's a miracle. Think about it. The two of you are actually talking to the God of the universe! Jesus Christ is there with you in a personal way, and the Holy Spirit is also present.

I have one word for you: *pray*. Actually, two words: *pray together*. Okay, make it three words: *pray together regularly*. Praying together regularly will improve every single area of your relationship, because when you pray, the three members of the Godhead are with you!

## Pray before You Talk

I recommend that every married couple set aside twenty to thirty minutes every day for face-to-face, no-distractions-allowed talk time. But just carving out the time isn't enough. If you want great conversations, pray before you talk. Jesus will help you open up. Even a few short minutes of prayer is a great way to jump-start a conversation.

You know how difficult it can be to start a conversation. There you are, just the two of you, staring at each other. You can hear the hum of the refrigerator and the drip of the kitchen faucet as you search for something to say. How do you shift gears from the hassles of the day—work, kids, home maintenance, bills—to a time of sharing and dialogue? How do you slip past your male-female differences? How do you get a conversation off the ground?

The answer is that you pray together first. It's the perfect ice-breaker. When you start a conversation with prayer, it gets you both in the mood to communicate. You are automatically on a deeper level, so when you start talking, you're already beneath the surface. You're warmed up. You're more open and more vulnerable.

During prayer, it's often easier to open up and share personally. It can be extremely difficult, especially for a husband, to reveal something personal directly to his wife. I mean she's sitting there staring at him! There's nowhere to hide! Will she laugh? Worse yet, will she ask a million questions and want you to probe even deeper?

For a man, it's often easier to express something personal in a pretalk prayer. His eyes are closed. More importantly, his wife's eyes are closed. She can't give an immediate reaction because it's rude to interrupt someone who is praying. He can collect his thoughts and feelings and express them in a more controlled, less pressured situation.

Half the battle for a man is just getting something personal out of his mouth. Prayer will help get it out. Later, in the talk time, he can go into more detail about what he mentioned in prayer. Eventually, he'll be able to tell his wife directly what's inside.

When you pray before you talk, God reaches out and deepens your level of conversation. He looks down from heaven and sees you praying—actually, through Christ, He's there with you on the couch—and He says: "I like this. I like this a lot. I'm going to help these children of mine communicate, and I'm going to help them develop more intimacy."

I'm convinced that this is what happens. God is so pleased that you include Him in your talk time that He blesses you with intimacy. Because you have honored Him and drawn closer to Him, He just gives it to you.

## PRAY BEFORE YOU FIGHT

When you're dealing with a conflict and feelings of anger are running high, prayer is especially important. I realize that when you're angry, praying is the last thing you want to do. But it ought to be the *first* thing you do. God wants to help you and your spouse get through the conflict and be closer at the end. But you've got to involve Him. Without His help, a lot of things can and will go wrong in an argument.

I urge you to pray together briefly before you begin talking through a problem. And, of course, avoid using prayer to take potshots at your partner: *Dear Lord, help Patty with her temper; she can be so mean and petty* or *God, please change Jim's heart and show him how misguided he is.* Pray for God to be with you as you resolve the conflict, to give you the ability to understand your partner's point of view, to accept and care about his or her feelings, and to be open to compromise.

Pray before an argument: *God, help us to work through this in a healthy, constructive way.* Take a break during an argument and pray: *God, give us guidance and perseverance to truly resolve this.*

After the argument pray: *Dear Father, thank you for being with us.* With God's presence and assistance, you can fight fairly and settle any dispute.

## PRAY BEFORE SEX

I know this suggestion may strike some people as odd, but taking a few minutes to pray before sex can make the experience much more passionate and fulfilling. As I said in chapter 6, God invented sex, and He wants married couples to enjoy sexual intimacy. So why not ask for His help and blessing? Prayer is great preparation for sexual intimacy. Since prayer has a way of binding two hearts together, you're already emotionally connected on a deeper level. A word of caution to men: Don't use prayer as a way to get sex. Believe me, your wife will catch on. Rather, lead her in prayer on a regular basis, and good sex will be a nice side effect.

## PRAY BEFORE EVERY ACTIVITY

No matter what you do as a couple, you want God along, don't you? God wants to be involved in your every activity. When you take a few minutes to pray and invite Him along, you'll sense His presence. Whatever you're doing will go better. It's particularly important to pray before an activity that will be difficult, painful, or challenging. Life is full of experiences like these. Don't face them without God.

One couple I saw for therapy was working on overcoming their negative, critical pattern of interaction. I told them that they were in desperate need of some positive time together. So I gave them a homework assignment: Take a walk together every evening, making sure that the conversation is positive, upbeat, and uplifting. Absolutely no negatives or conflict on these walks, I said.

Despite their good intentions, reality quickly set in. On their first happy, positive walk, their old argumentative streak reared its ugly head. They had a fight over some insignificant issue. The wife sped up and walked twenty feet ahead...on the opposite side of the street. They walked around the block that way.

I laughed when they told me this ridiculous story. I said: "Maybe you didn't understand me. The idea was for you to walk *together.*"

I went to plan B. I told them to pray before their walks—to ask Jesus to be with them and to help them get around the block without World War III breaking out. I asked them to picture Jesus walking with them. They did pray, and it began to change the way they talked as they took their stroll each day. They became less defensive and slower to point out faults in each other. They said that picturing Jesus listening in on their conversations motivated them to be more patient and encouraging.

Yes, this couple still had months of hard work to do in therapy. They learned how to communicate, how to fight fair, and how to rekindle their romantic feelings. But it was the brief prayers before their walks that started their improved interaction. They began to pray at other times during the week: in the morning before they left for work, on the phone when something important came up, and prior to their talk times in the evening. Prayer became one of the hallmarks of their marriage, and it remains so today.

Whatever the circumstances of your marriage—whether you're trying to overcome some problems or just seeking to improve an already healthy relationship—prayer will foster deeper intimacy and protect you from the enemy's attacks. In Ephesians 6:18, Paul instructs us to "pray at all times." I believe that this applies not just to individual Christians, but also to married couples who love the Lord Jesus Christ and seek His protection from the devil. Satan would like nothing more than for you to have a stale, lackluster, lifeless marriage. He never stops trying to cripple and destroy your relationship. When you and your spouse make prayer a regular part of your life, you establish a shield around you. What's more, you tap into the power of God, which helps fuse you as a couple.

# 12

# SETTING A COURSE

How to Pray As a Couple

'I've said to thousands of Christian husbands and wives: "Tell me about your prayer life as a couple." Sadly, these have been very brief conversations. The majority—about 99 percent—responded in the same way: "Well, Dave, we really don't pray together much at all. We pray before meals, but that's usually as a family. We pray silently in church as we sit together. When there's a crisis and we really need the Lord's help, we pray together."

These couples know that they should pray together. They know that it would help their relationship. They even *want* to pray together. So why don't they? One of the main reasons is that they don't know how. You may scoff, "How could a couple not know how to pray together? All you do is kneel beside the couch together and talk to God. It's not too complicated." True, but praying as a couple is different from and far more difficult than praying alone. It doesn't come naturally. Many couples feel awkward and self-conscious praying together. So in this chapter, I offer a few suggestions and guidelines for getting your collective prayer life going. If you and your spouse already pray together, perhaps these ideas will help you to maximize your prayer times.

## Don't Leave It to Chance

The first thing you must do is *schedule* your prayer times each week. Do not—I repeat, do not—take this approach: "Yeah, honey, let's pray a few times this week. Maybe before we head off to work or after we get the kids into bed. We'll just play it by ear and see how the week goes." Don't kid yourselves. If you don't nail down specific times, you won't pray. Your own resistance, Satan's opposition, and the hectic rush of life will thwart your plans.

Sit down on Saturday or Sunday and plan your prayer sessions for the upcoming week. Pinpoint the exact days and times. These are important appointments—appointments with your spouse and God—so you put them on your calendar. Schedule them in like any other meeting or activity. You don't want to forget. God will be waiting for you, and you don't want to stand Him up, do you?

Pick the times that are best for you. Some couples prefer praying in the morning. If you have children still living at home, forget the morning. At our house, mornings are a mad blur of making life-and-death decisions about clothes (you can tell I have daughters), crunching cereal, stuffing schoolbooks into fifty-pound backpacks, and shouting good-byes. The only prayer that Sandy and I have time for is a quick, silent plea: "Dear God, please get these kids out of the house and out of our hair."

For most couples, evening is the best time to pray. Just make sure that you schedule your sessions as early in the evening as possible. You want to pray when you are fresh and still have some brain cells operating. You have a window of opportunity, usually one to one and a half hours, between dinner/kid time and your bedtime. Don't wait until you're exhausted and ready to collapse into bed. Give the best you have to God and to each other.

For couples just beginning to pray together regularly, I suggest that you pray together for five minutes three times a week. Once or twice a week just isn't enough to get into a consistent, committed pattern. As I recommended previously, it's a good idea to schedule prayer just before your daily twenty- to thirty-minute talk time. This helps you remember to pray and is a terrific way to warm up for conversation. You may eventually pray before every talk time, which would mean seven brief prayers each week.

Also, choose one special place in your home to pray. This will probably be the same place you use to talk. After your prayer, it's easier to just stay where you are and segue into conversation. You need a private, quiet spot where you will not be distracted or disturbed in any way. If you have children, confine them to their rooms or a certain part of the house during your time together. And do not pray in bed. A quiet time in bed will be quiet all right, since you might just fall asleep!

When you pray, hold hands. This connects you in a warm and loving way. It is a beautiful picture of unity, and it reminds you that you are becoming one flesh. It has a way of lowering defenses and helping you both reach a deeper level of openness and vulnerability. And please, pray out loud. It defeats the purpose of spiritual bonding to pray silently, even if you're sitting right next to each other. If you don't know what your partner is saying to God, you can't know him or her spiritually. There is no connection, no sharing. There will be times of silence, and in the beginning you may not pray on a deep, personal level. But you need to pray out loud most of the time so that you can draw closer to each other as you grow closer to God.

## TAKING TURNS IN PRAYER

You've scheduled a five-minute prayer time. You're sitting together in your special place, holding hands. Now what? The best way to begin is to pray for things you have agreed on in advance. Bring up prayer concerns—children, relatives, friends, your church's ministries, job problems, health issues—and develop a list. Decide what to pray for, divide the list between you, and pray—one partner at a time—for several minutes. First, the man prays, then the woman prays, until you've worked through your list of requests and praises. This may not be the most intimate kind of prayer, but it will help you get going in the right direction.

You should continue to pray in this way for several months. As you go along, both of you will find it easier to be more open and personal in your prayers. You'll be sharing more details about your individual lives—things you're concerned about, things you are thankful for, things God is teaching you. In time, you can move from *reporting* these details to expressing your emotions about the details. Go from the general to the specific, from the superficial to the deep.

For example, a man might mention in his prayer that he's having a problem at work. He just keeps it general, so his wife has no idea what's really happening. She wants to ask what the problem is, but she holds off. She knows that it was hard for him to admit the problem at all. A few weeks later, he describes in more detail his work situation. He tells God (and his wife, indirectly) that his supervisor is badgering him, and he asks for patience and strength to deal with this person. A week later the husband might finally feel comfortable enough to open up and share his feelings of frustration, anger, and helplessness about his ongoing predicament. After that prayer, they have a good talk about his problem at work.

## CONVERSATIONAL PRAYER

After a number of months, probably five or six at least, you'll be able to pray conversationally. This is a deeper level, and it takes time to get there. Hand in hand with your eyes closed, you take turns talking to God. You still have a basic list of prayer items, but you don't each pray for a certain predetermined number of them. You just start and go back and forth. The man prays a few sentences, the woman prays a few sentences, and then the man prays again—on and on, just like a normal conversation. The only difference is that God is also present. It's a three-way conversation.

Conversational prayer is free flowing, spontaneous, and personal. You don't worry about what specific things you are supposed to pray for. You mention anything and everything that comes to mind. You respond to each other. You may repeat what your partner prays. You may add to what your partner prays. Something your spouse prays may trigger something in your mind, and you'll pray about that. You don't know where you're going in your prayers, and that's fine. That's the idea. You just let it happen.

When you pray conversationally, you allow the Holy Spirit much more room to maneuver and influence what's happening. You're open to His guidance and direction. He could take you anywhere. It's up to Him. The exciting thing is that it's not you who are praying, but God giving you the words through the Holy Spirit. As the apostle Paul says in Romans 8:26: "In the same way the Spirit also helps our weakness; for we do not know how to pray as we should, but the Spirit Himself intercedes for us with groanings too deep for words." Have you ever wondered, as I have, what this verse really means? You'll find out in conversational prayer. There's no experience quite like the Spirit moving in your prayer time.

At first, you may pray conversationally about safe topics. As you get the hang of it, you'll pray about personal things: needs, worries, pain, joys, victories. Then you'll pray about your relationship in an honest and vulnerable way. One spouse will mention a need, and the other spouse will pray for God's help to meet that need. You can communicate on the deepest possible level because you have the Holy Spirit Himself moving between you and giving you the words to say.

To give you a glimpse of what conversational prayer is like, I've included a brief excerpt from one couple's prayer time:

**Wife:** *Dear Father, I'm concerned about our daughter, Susan. She's attracted to a boy who doesn't know You.*

**Husband:** *God, I'm worried about my little girl, too. She's sixteen, but I still want to protect her. Father, please keep her safe. Help her to see that this young man is not good for her.*

**Wife:** *I echo what Dan just said. And, Father, help us to be strong and close in our marriage. We need to stay united to deal effectively with Susan and the other kids.*

**Husband:** *Sharon's right, Lord. We need to be close as a couple, but lately that hasn't been the case. I've been too busy at work. I need to be at home more with Sharon and the kids. And, Lord, I know Sharon has been very tired these past few months. Give her strength.*

**Wife:** *Thank You, Lord, for helping us both see the need to get back on track as a couple. I have been tired, and I think it's because I'm overcommitted at church and at the kids' school. Show me where to cut back.*

**Husband:** *Father, hearing Sharon pray makes me realize that we're just too busy. We do need to back off of some things. I know I've skipped quite a few quiet times with You in the last two weeks.*

**Wife:** *Please, Lord, give Dan wisdom about how to handle his schedule and all his demands. We all need him to be our leader and....*

You see how it works? Dan and Sharon start out praying for their daughter, move to their marriage, and then to their personal and spiritual lives. With the Holy Spirit's guidance, this conversational prayer could go any number of places. It will go where the Spirit wants it to go.

## THE STORB APPROACH

Sandy and I have discovered a simple and effective way to pray. I call it the STORB approach because the letters of this acronym describe the five stages we move through when we pray:

- I'm Sorry
- Thank You, Lord
- Observations
- Requests
- Bridge to Conversation

This approach works best when you are praying conversationally, so it will take a little while to learn these stages and feel comfortable with the progression. But I think that you will like our model and find that it enriches your prayer life. Let me explain how it works.

*S: I'm Sorry*

Your prayer time begins with confession of your sins. This always ought to come first because it's important to enter God's presence clean and forgiven. You don't want anything to get in the way and block open communication with God. Unconfessed sins get in the way, as Psalm 66:18 states: "If I regard wickedness in my heart, the Lord will not hear."

You each spend a minute or two silently confessing any sins that are particularly personal or embarrassing. There's no need to expose these to your partner—just to God. The partner who finishes first gently squeezes the other person's hand. When the other partner has finished, his squeeze signals that you're both ready to move into verbal confession.

Now you each confess out loud to God personal sins and "couple sins." By couple sins, I mean sins you've committed against your spouse. If you've done or said something that has hurt your mate, confess it and ask God's forgiveness. You'll have to discuss these couple sins later, in your talk time, but you receive God's forgiveness first and start the process of forgiveness between the two of you.

It may take some time before you get comfortable confessing your sins out loud. It requires a deep level of trust and vulnerability. At first, this stage will be largely silent prayer. You'll both confess just to God, squeeze hands to indicate when you're done, and move to the next stage. But with time, you'll grow closer and feel comfortable with confessing your sins aloud.

I think you'll find that it's easier to first express your couple sins in prayer instead of face-to-face in direct conversation. Somehow you won't feel as threatened or be as defensive when you're telling God how you've hurt your spouse. Again, you don't use this as a method to avoid working through a conflict: "Honey, I'm not going to talk about that. You heard me confess it to the Lord, and I'm forgiven." Nice try, but it doesn't work that way. You will talk about the issue later in conversation, but it will be easier to resolve because you have confessed it to God.

### T: Thank You, Lord

Next, you each thank God for all He is doing for you and praise Him for His goodness. In Colossians 4:2, Paul tells Christians to "devote yourselves to prayer, keeping alert in it with an attitude of thanksgiving." God loves to be praised! When we praise Him, He draws close to us. God is "enthroned upon" the praises of His people (Psalm 22:3).

A healthy Christian couple praises God frequently, especially for the gift of His Son. If sending Jesus to earth to die for our sins was all God ever did for us, that alone would be enough for us to praise Him forever. The amazing truth is that God continues to give and give and give. He showers us with countless blessings out of His infinite grace. As James 1:17 says, "Every good thing bestowed and every perfect gift is from above, coming down from the Father of lights."

What do we do in response to God's never-ending grace and generosity? We thank Him and praise Him! In this second stage of prayer, take a few minutes to praise God for your salvation, for your precious spouse, for family and friends, for health and income, and for answered prayers. Thank Him for all that He has done for you in the past, for what He's doing in the present, and for what He is yet to do. As you give God praise and thanks, your hearts will be warmed and invigorated and opened—to Him and to each other.

### O: Observations

In the third stage of your couple prayer time, you go a little deeper and get a little more personal. I call this level *observations* because you tell God what you see happening in your life. It's a quick "state-of-your-life" update. You talk to God about the good things that are going on. You talk about the things that aren't so good. You review with Him how you're doing spiritually, emotionally, and physically. You describe the stresses and concerns you're facing. You mention any problems you're having in your marriage.

About now, you might be thinking, *Man, this is pretty personal!* You're right. It is. You would ordinarily share these kinds of observations only in your private prayer time with God, right? I'm suggesting that, with time and practice, you can let your marriage partner see what's really, genuinely going on in your life. You'll start off with rather superficial observations about your life and relationship. Then you'll get more specific and more vulnerable. Most couples who pray together spend most of their time asking God for things. That's better than not praying at all, but it doesn't create spiritual intimacy. Don't settle for a safe, predictable prayer life. Go deeper!

When you hit your stride in this stage, you'll be revealing who you really are and how you're really doing in the key areas of your life. This kind of openness and honesty will help you grow spiritually as a person, and it will lead to a deeper spiritual bond with your mate.

## R: Requests

The apostle Paul gives us the biblical principle for this stage: "Do not be anxious about anything, but in everything, by prayer and petition, with thanksgiving, present your requests to God" (Philippians 4:6, NIV). God wants us to bring Him *all* of our requests. The words *in everything* mean that the sky's the limit. As you pray together, lay before God your needs and concerns—small things, big things, scary things, confusing things.

God will listen and answer your prayers. Jesus promised that when two or three Christians join in prayer about anything, He is there with them, and His Father will answer that prayer (Matthew 18:19–20). Of course, the answer you get will be up to God. It will be according to His will. When you and your mate offer your requests, you'll feel the peace that is beyond human understanding, which comes from knowing the outcome is in God's hands. You'll feel the presence of Jesus. You'll be able to rest in Christ's promise that God will answer. It's a great way to end your prayer time.

## B: Bridge to Conversation

But wait! You're not done yet. There's a fifth stage—the bridge to conversation—that is critical for developing spiritual intimacy. Here, you won't be praying; you'll be talking. I include this stage in my STORB model because it is the natural extension of your prayer time. As you move through the first four stages, you are doing two important things: First and foremost, you are growing closer to God and each other; second, you are making the best possible preparation for your talk time.

In each of these stages, you have developed a rich mine of conversational material. When you finish the fourth stage and open your eyes, you have built a bridge from each stage to your time of communication. You start talking about the topics you just prayed about. You can flow naturally and seamlessly from prayer to conversation.

To illustrate how this stage works, let's take a look at the topics one couple generated in the first four stages of prayer:

**Sorry**
Husband yelled at coworker
Wife missed three days of personal devotions
Husband watched sports on TV all day on Sunday
Wife was cold and withdrawn for two days
**Thank You**
Our church and the new ministry we're involved with
Our daughter making a good friend at school
The healing of a family member
**Observations**
Husband feeling stress at work
Wife in a dry spiritual time
Romance lacking in the marriage
Satan attacking us more lately
**Requests**
Continued recovery of family member
Guidance for husband at work
Spiritual vitality for wife
God's leading in our new church ministry

Do you see what I mean about conversational material? This list is jam-packed with topics for this couple to discuss. The only problem will be in deciding which issues to focus on. When married couples moan to me that they don't have anything to talk about, I ask them, "Do you pray together first?" They usually mutter, "Well, no," and then ask, "What do you mean, praying together first?" I explain my STORB approach. Couples who practice these stages report that, after a month or two, their conversations are greatly improved.

When you follow the STORB stages of prayer, you become open, closer, and ready to communicate. Best of all, you have God with you to help you talk. You build a bridge from spiritual intimacy to emotional intimacy. And when you create spiritual and emotional intimacy, you are ready for physical intimacy as well. You can get the whole package. And it all starts with prayer.

# GO FOR THE GOLD

*Don't Settle for Second Best in Your Prayer Life*

About six months ago, Sandy and I realized that, although we were doing well in our prayer times together, we could do even better. We had been using the ideas I've described in the previous two chapters, and they were working for us. We felt close to each other and to God. Nothing was wrong, but we thirsted for a deeper, richer prayer life.

Like every couple, Sandy and I have strengths and weaknesses in our relationship. One of our strengths, I'm happy to say, is that we don't settle for the merely acceptable, comfortable, or middle-of-the-road. We may settle for a while, but when we notice that that's what we're doing, we make changes. That's how it was with our prayer times.

Why not strive to be the best you can possibly be? The athletes who compete in the Olympic games always want the gold medal. You never hear a world-class athlete say, "I'd be happy if I got the bronze medal" or "This time I'm aiming for the silver—that'll be enough." No way! They go for the gold. In our own way, Sandy and I were like these athletes. We didn't want to be satisfied with the bronze or silver medal in our prayer life.

If you follow the principles in chapters 11 and 12, you'll develop a good prayer life together—a better one than most couples have. But, like Sandy and me, you may realize that it could be even more powerful, meaningful, and intimate.

To reach this deeper level of prayer, you need to add to the STORB framework the steps I describe in the next few pages. These steps will require time, effort, and commitment from both of you. But you'll find that the payoff is more than worth it. Do what Paul exhorted the Thessalonian believers to do: "Excel still more" (1 Thessalonians 4:1). Don't be satisfied with the bronze medal in your prayer life. Go for the gold!

## Pray with the Spirit

Praying alone, as an individual, can be difficult. Praying together, as a couple, can be even more difficult. Who will help you get over the initial resistance and awkwardness as you begin praying together? Who will teach you how to pray? Who will direct and energize your prayer times? The Holy Spirit will. That's one of His main jobs! You can have the Holy Spirit as your supernatural prayer guide every time you and your partner pray.

In fact, it's quite easy to know for certain that you have the Spirit as your prayer guide. All you have to do is ask God. It's just that simple. Right at the end of the "I'm Sorry" stage—after you've confessed your personal and relationship sins—ask God, out loud, to fill you with the Holy Spirit. First, pray to be filled individually. Second, pray that the Spirit will direct both of you, speak through you, and make you one as you pray.

You and I know that it's important to "walk by the Spirit" individually (Romans 8:4; Galatians 5:16, 25). But it's also important to walk *together* by the Spirit. One of the best ways to walk by the Spirit as a couple is to invite Him into your prayer times. When you both confess your sins and ask for the Spirit's filling, He will be present in a powerful way.

## KEEP YOUR EARS OPEN

In our prayer life together, Sandy and I have been guilty of getting stuck in the monologue mode. Time after time, we've prayed the same old tired lines. We've confessed the same two or three sins, thanked God for the standard blessings, rattled off the usual list of requests, and said "Amen." When we slip into this rut, prayer is just another duty to check off the list. There's no life, no real passion, in the experience. Frankly, it's boring—to me, to Sandy, and (I presume) to God.

The problem with this kind of prayer is that it's one-way communication. We're the only ones talking; we don't listen to God. We don't wait to hear what He has to say. Sandy and I get back on track when we realize that we need to let God respond. Prayer is a dialogue. It's two-way communication. What kind of relationship would Sandy and I have if I did all the talking and never listened to what she had to say? We build a relationship with God in prayer by talking *and* listening to Him.

Part of the excitement in your prayer times will be the unpredictability. What is God going to say to you? What is He going to impress upon you? How is He going to guide your prayer time? When you are both quiet and listen to God, He'll talk to you. Although you may not hear an audible voice (that's never happened to Sandy and me), God will communicate to you through the Holy Spirit.

In the past few months, Sandy and I have heard some specific things from God in our prayer times. I heard God gently urging me to help Sandy more around the house. He helped me see that she was tired and burdened. God also impressed upon me that I needed to spend more time with my daughters, Emily, Leeann, and Nancy. I had gotten so involved with my son, William, that I'd been neglecting the girls. My heavenly Father reminded me that the girls need their earthly dad, too.

Over the course of several weeks of praying together, Sandy got the clear message from God that she should become a leader in the Pioneer Club program at our church. Working with young girls is one of her strengths, and God wanted her to use it. Sandy also heard God prompting her to reach out to one of our daughter's schoolteachers. He kept bringing this lady to her mind in our prayer times. She felt strongly that God wanted her to invite this woman to our church and build a relationship with her. She followed through, and God has blessed their growing relationship.

As Sandy and I have learned, listening to God allows Him to guide and direct us. I love the imagery Jesus used to describe the relationship we are to have with Him:

> The sheep hear his voice, and he calls his own sheep by name, and leads them out. When he puts forth all his own, he goes before them, and the sheep follow him because they know his voice. (John 10:3–4)

We are the sheep, and Jesus is the shepherd. If we listen, we will know His voice and be able to follow Him.

In your prayer times, take a few minutes to be quiet and listen. You can pause and listen in the "I'm Sorry" stage as you ask God to bring to your mind the sins and omissions you need to confess. You can listen in the "Thank You" stage, and He will reveal the blessings for which He wants you to express appreciation. You can also pause briefly in the "Observations" and "Requests" stages to hear what God has to say. Like every good conversation, prayer has moments of quiet reflection. So start listening. God has some things to say to you.

## ALLOW MORE TIME FOR PRAYER

After you've been praying for a few months, you'll probably start feeling a desire to spend a little more time talking and listening to God. You'll realize that, even though it's productive and valuable, praying a couple of times a week for five or ten minutes isn't enough to reach a deeper level of intimacy with God. You need more time in prayer to apply the "go for the gold" principles in this chapter. I believe that you need a twenty- to thirty-minute period each week to really stretch your prayer muscles and fully implement all the prayer strategies I'm giving you.

This once-a-week session, which I call a spiritual evaluation session, will become one of the highlights of your spiritual bonding experience. In addition to having an extended prayer time, you'll use this session for other spiritual activities: reading the Bible, spiritual conversations, accountability, and worship. It's a good idea to schedule this meeting near the end of the week. That way, you can pray and talk about the things that happened that week. If you've been busy and missed opportunities to pray and talk about spiritual things, you can use this time to catch up and reconnect.

## KEEP A PRAYER JOURNAL

One of the most useful tools in a couple's prayer life is a prayer journal. This is an excellent way to keep track of your prayers and God's answers. Life is complicated and busy, and it's hard for most of us to retain all the information that's thrown our way. If you don't write down the items you want to pray about, you may forget them. You might pray a few times for a certain person or situation, but all too soon the onrushing current of life can sweep this important prayer concern out of your minds.

Try this journaling system: Buy two notebooks—one for current prayer requests and one for long-range prayer requests. In the first notebook, list the urgent, pressing needs you are bringing to God. Typically, you're looking for answers to these requests in a matter of days or weeks. In the second notebook, jot down requests that you expect to be lifting up to God for quite some time, such as the salvation of a family member or the health problems of a chronically ill person.

Regularly update both these lists by checking with the people you're praying for. Doing so enables you to pray more specifically and intelligently for their changing needs. When you get these updates, write the new information in your journals.

There will be a continual ebb and flow in these two journals. When it becomes obvious that a current item will require continued prayer, you should transfer it to the long-range list. As time goes on, God will answer requests on both lists. When you receive an answer, write it in a third notebook—your *Book of Answered Prayer*. You can use a hardbound book with blank pages for this purpose. It's exciting to keep a written record of God's faithfulness in answered prayers. From time to time, you can bring out this special book and review the many answers God has provided over your years of praying together. When life is painful and faith and hope are in short supply, get out your *Book of Answered Prayer* and start reading.

## KNEEL IN PRAYER

Remember the couple I described in chapter 11? The ones who were sure that their marriage was over until they began their three-hour prayer vigil? They told me that they had knelt during this marriage-changing time of prayer and that being on their knees seemed to make a difference. I've heard the same report from other couples. Periodically, Sandy and I kneel in prayer, and it always adds an extra something special to the experience.

As couples we should take literally and seriously the apostle Paul's example of kneeling in prayer (see Ephesians 3:14). When we do, we acknowledge God's holiness and majesty. By going *down* on our knees, we can more readily picture God *up* on His throne. In Psalm 95:6 the psalmist urges us to come before the Lord our Maker in this position of worship and reverence. Although I don't think that we need to kneel every time we pray, when we do, we demonstrate that we are helpless, humble, and respectful. Indeed, it is difficult to be proud or arrogant on bended knees.

## FASTING AND PRAYING

Most Christians aren't very big on fasting. We're big on eating. Just try to get people to turn out for a church meeting with this announcement: "There will be no food, just a time of worship and prayer." You probably wouldn't have to worry about an overflow crowd. We like to add food, huge mounds of food, to our spiritual gatherings. We feel that before we can worship, we have to eat donuts, coffee cake, pie, or that wonderful chicken broccoli casserole Mrs. Brubaker makes.

I'm not saying that it's wrong to eat as part of a spiritual meeting. I like to eat as much as the next person. I'm saying that it's easy to allow food to get in the way of a real connection with God. This is particularly true in your prayer life. When you're eating three squares a day, you're focused on yourself and meeting the need of wanting to eat. When you're not eating for a period of time and devoting yourself to prayer, you can focus solely on God.

In both the Old and New Testaments, numerous references are made to fasting and praying. They go together. Nehemiah fasted and prayed (Nehemiah 1:4). Daniel fasted and prayed (Daniel 9:3). David fasted and prayed (Psalm 35:13). Paul, Barnabas, and a group of church leaders fasted and prayed (Acts 13:2–3). In each case, these godly men fasted and prayed in times of great difficulty, stress, and preparation for some major spiritual undertaking.

All I can say is that if these heavyweights of the faith fasted and prayed, it must be a good idea for us as well. And not just as individuals, but as married couples. Fasting and praying together will create a powerful spiritual experience. You don't have to fast for forty days like Jesus did. Just miss a few meals occasionally in preparation for a prayer time.

The discipline of fasting and praying is especially effective when life is difficult and painful—when you have to make a crucial decision, when something bad has happened, or when you desperately need God's comfort and guidance. At times like these, skip meals together for a day, and go to your knees in prayer. When the distractions of life are screened out, you will be attuned to God's voice. You will be acutely aware of His presence. Both of you will hunger and thirst only for God. And He will satisfy you.

## PRAY LIKE CHILDREN

If you've ever listened to children pray, you know how precious it is to hear the way they approach God—openly, honestly, directly, without pretense or desire to impress. Children come to God exactly as they are, with their thoughts, feelings, insecurities, and needs laid bare.

Jesus loves children, and during His earthly ministry, He welcomed them into His presence (Mark 10:13–16). He held up their simple, innocent faith as an example to all Christians.

I believe that God loves it when we pray like children. No flowery, eloquent speeches. No efforts to impress Him or our partner. Just the clear, uncomplicated words of children talking to their trusted Father.

It is especially important for the more spiritually mature spouse to pray in a childlike way. You might easily intimidate and discourage your spouse if you launch into some deeply theological, articulate, long-winded prayer. Keep it simple and straightforward, just like a child. This approach will please the Lord and make your less-experienced partner feel comfortable and willing to continue praying with you.

When you put into practice all of the suggestions presented in this chapter, you and your spouse will be on your way to becoming champions of prayer. Don't settle for a *good* prayer life when you could have a *great* one. Don't settle for the silver medal when you could have the gold.

# PLUGGED INTO
# THE POWER

*Reading God's Word Together*

*I* was sitting with a man and his wife in my office. It was near the end of the therapy session, and we were discussing the spiritual aspect of their relationship. They admitted that they both were spiritually flat.

"We don't feel close to God," the husband said. "We can't figure out His will for our lives and relationship. We're just not experiencing His power in our marriage."

"How often do you read the Bible?" I asked.

The man thought for a moment, then said, "To be honest, I read the Bible about twice a week."

"And I usually read it three times a week," the wife responded.

"No, you don't understand. I mean, how often do you read the Bible *together*?"

They looked at each other, back at me, and finally the wife replied, "Well, actually, we don't read the Bible together."

I shared with them my conviction that reading the Bible together is a primary means of accessing God's power. I tried to persuade them that reading the Word of God regularly would invigorate the spiritual part of their relationship. It would bring them closer to God. It would make His will for their marriage clear. It would give them a collective energy boost.

I didn't give this husband and wife a hard time for not reading the Bible together. In fact, I told them that I could relate to their situation. I admitted that my wife and I didn't read the Bible together for years. We didn't realize what we were missing. We didn't know that we were choosing to leave a huge power source untapped. It was like trying to operate our home without any electricity. We were running our marriage manually, using just our own energy, and it didn't work too well.

I told this couple about the Bible reading program that Sandy and I have developed, and they decided to try it. Over the course of two months, they sat down and read God's Word together. They discussed the passages they read, and they helped each other apply them. Simply put, they allowed the Bible's power to transform their marriage.

At the end of the two months, they were much closer to God and to each other. They had found the power to communicate, to resolve conflict, and to love each other much more deeply. This obvious yet profound spiritual discipline provided the rejuvenation this couple so sorely needed.

## Training, Exposing, Nourishing

I urge you to plug into the power of the Word of God. The Bible is your training guide for living the Christian life: "All Scripture is God-breathed and is useful for teaching, rebuking, correcting and training in righteousness, so that the man of God may be thoroughly equipped for every good work" (2 Timothy 3:16–17, NIV).

Reading and studying the Bible together will bring down your walls and reveal who you really are. God's Word will cut through every defense and barrier. As Hebrews 4:12 says, "For the word of God is living and active and sharper than any two-edged sword, and piercing as far as the division of soul and spirit, of both joints and marrow, and able to judge the thoughts and intentions of the heart."

Genuine closeness between a husband and wife comes only when their hearts are revealed—when they express their real thoughts, motivations, and emotions. How do you reach this deep level of vulnerability and openness? One of the best ways is by reading the Bible together. God promises you a life of prosperity and success if you faithfully study and follow His Word:

> But his delight is in the law of the LORD, and in His law he meditates day and night. And he will be like a tree firmly planted by streams of water, Which yields its fruit in its season, And its leaf does not wither; And in whatever he does, he prospers. (Psalm 1:2–3)

I believe that this promise applies not just to individual believers, but also to Christian married couples. If you commit to read the Word of God together regularly, you will be like two trees firmly planted by streams of water. The Bible will be a continual source of nourishment and vitality for your relationship.

## GET THE TOOLS

To get started, all you need are two basic tools. First, you each need a good study Bible. Select one with helpful notes that give the historical context, explain the meaning of key verses, and list other verses on the same topic. If you're a new Christian, it may be wise to choose a modern, easy-to-read translation, such as the New International Version.

The second tool is a good Bible commentary on the Old and New Testaments. This is an invaluable aid in understanding and gaining insight into God's Word. As you read Scripture, you can refer to your commentary for a wealth of information: a verse-by-verse exposition, the meanings of key Hebrew and Greek words, background of authorship, book outline, the purpose of each book, and the central themes found in each. (I highly recommend the two-volume commentary set written by faculty members of Dallas Theological Seminary: *The Bible Knowledge Commentary*, Old Testament and New Testament editions.)

## ONE PASSAGE AT A TIME

To make your time together in the Bible profitable, you should read slowly and carefully. Read and study one short passage (one verse or several verses) at a time. Concentrate on the passage, linger on it, and try to discern what God is teaching you through His Word.

Speed isn't important. Understanding and application are important. Some couples have told me proudly, "We're reading through the Bible together in one year!" My response has been: "That's great. What are you learning?" Too often, they can't answer me. It defeats the purpose to race through Scripture at breakneck speed. When you read too many verses at a time, you risk putting your mind on autopilot. You're not engaged with what God is telling you. Zero in on one specific section, and take it slowly.

## THERE'S PLENTY OF MATERIAL

There are a variety of ways to choose Bible passages to read and study. Your individual quiet times with God can call your attention to verses that you might want to look at further with your partner. As you read your Bible alone, the Holy Spirit might use a certain verse to convict you. Jot down that verse and share it with your spouse at your next Bible reading session.

Your pastor's sermons are a gold mine of verses for your Bible study. Take advantage of the hours he has spent researching and studying. Use his understanding of the Hebrew and the Greek.

Take notes on his interpretation of a Scripture passage, and talk about that passage during the week.

Some time ago, my pastor, Kirk Johnston, gave a convicting message on forgiveness. As his text, he used the words of Jesus recorded in Matthew:

> Therefore, if you are offering your gift at the altar and there remember that your brother has something against you, leave your gift there in front of the altar. First go and be reconciled to your brother; then come and offer your gift. (Matthew 5:23–24, NIV)

The Holy Spirit was speaking to my heart, and I knew what I had to do. Right after the service, I asked a man and his wife to forgive me for something careless and hurtful I had done to them two years earlier. They graciously forgave me. I told Sandy about it, and we used this passage in Matthew that week in our Bible reading sessions.

Sunday school lessons are another rich source of discussion material. If a passage your teacher uses for a lesson is timely and powerful, take it as a subject for reading and studying with your partner. Radio Bible teachers can also be extremely helpful. I've taken a lot of verses from Chuck Swindoll's *Insight for Living* broadcast. That man can flat-out preach, and he handles the Bible superbly. You can listen to Chuck in the morning on the way to work and come back home that evening with a verse or two for you and your mate to study.

It's okay to read and study passages from different books in the Bible. One week you may be in Matthew, the next week in 1 Corinthians, then in Daniel, and so on. But I recommend that you spend at least half of your study time reading a book of the Bible from beginning to end. You just take small chunks, a few verses at a time. This approach provides continuity and a smoother flow of Scripture. You'll get a good, solid picture of the book's overall message and purpose, and you won't have to worry about which passage you'll read next because you'll just pick up where you left off.

If you're new to Bible reading and studying as a couple, there are certain books of the Bible I suggest you start with. With its beautiful language and short, wisdom-filled verses about life and relationships, Proverbs is a great book for couples. Paul's epistles—Galatians, Ephesians, Philippians, and Colossians—are concise, easy to read, and intensely practical. I especially urge you to read the Gospels—Matthew, Mark, Luke, and John. Reading these accounts of Jesus' life and ministry is like sitting at the Master's feet as He teaches and enlightens.

## READ, MEDITATE, DISCUSS, APPLY

Reading the Bible together is a good thing, but don't stop there. Merely reading God's Word won't help you or your marriage. That would be like reading a recipe but not actually preparing a meal. It will not create a spiritual bond. The Bible provides us with God's instructions on how to live righteously in an unrighteous world, but it will do us no good if we don't apply it.

Do you want to be blessed—as an individual and as a married couple? Then read and study the Bible together and do what it says. We are to be "doers of the word, and not merely hearers" (James 1:22). If you decide to become doers, here's what happens:

> But one who looks intently at the perfect law, the law of liberty, and abides by it, not having become a forgetful hearer but an effectual doer, this man shall be blessed in what he does. (James 1:25)

Sandy and I have developed a simple, straightforward system for reading and studying the Bible. It doesn't take much time, and it takes into account the different ways that males and females communicate. It has helped us become better "doers of the Word." It works for us, and I think it will work for you. Working as a team, you follow four steps over a two-week period.

### Read

First, you sit down early in the week—on a Sunday or Monday evening—and one partner reads out loud the passage of Scripture you have selected. Typically, this reading occurs just after a prayer time. Take a moment or two to silently meditate on the passage. Let the Holy Spirit do His work. Then each of you briefly discusses your response to the passage. What does the passage mean? What is God saying to you through His Word? What thoughts or emotions does it trigger? To complete this step, each of you writes the passage on a three-by-five card.

### Meditate

During the next five or six days, you each carry your index card with you wherever you go. You might tape it to your pocket calendar, slip it into your wallet, or keep it in your purse. You read the verse at least once a day and meditate on it. This could be part of your daily, personal quiet time. You might do a little study of the verse, if that's necessary. Ask God to show you how He wants you to apply the verse. Be open to what He wants you to do, and jot down on the index card how you will apply it.

### Discuss

At the end of the week, meet again to share the results of the meditation and reflection. Tell each other what you will do to apply the passage in the coming week. Agree to write down on the back of the index card how you specifically applied the passage and what happened when you did. Pray briefly that God will help you to be doers of His Word.

*Apply*

The final step is to meet approximately one week later to share how God used the passage in each of your lives. You each read your comments about how you applied God's Word. You describe what you learned. You may have to admit that you didn't apply the verse and explain what hindered you from doing so. If either partner wasn't able to fully apply the passage, you extend the process another week.

Even when you have practiced this four-step process and gained some proficiency at it, it's unlikely that you will implement it in every two-week period of the year. That may be too much to expect. But reading and applying a passage once a month, or even once every two months, would be a tremendous accomplishment and greatly bless your relationship.

To illustrate this process, let's see how one married couple followed these four steps. The Scripture they used was Colossians 3:18–19: "Wives, be subject to your husbands, as is fitting in the Lord. Husbands, love your wives, and do not be embittered against them."

- *Read.* The wife reads the two verses out loud. Both partners silently meditate and then talk about the passage for a few minutes. The husband is pretty quiet. The wife shares how she has tried to be submissive in the past. She has more to say but wants to give him some time to process what she has already said. Each of them writes the verses on index cards.

- *Meditate.* As they read the verses and meditate on them over the next five days, both partners experience conviction. The husband realizes that he has resented his wife for spending too much time with their new baby. In retaliation, he has spent less time with her and has not listened to her talk about her needs and desires. The wife thinks about submission but hasn't yet come up with any specific way to apply this principle.

- **Discuss.** They meet on Friday evening, and the husband tells his wife about his resentment. He asks for her forgiveness and says that he will show his love to her this next week by giving her time and attention and listening to her talk. He spells out the specific evenings he will initiate these talk times. The wife admits coming up empty in her meditation process—until now. After hearing him share, she knows what to do to be submissive. She says that she will do her best to put the baby to bed a half-hour earlier each night and use that time to be with her husband.

- **Apply.** One week later, they come together again to talk about how they applied the passage that week. They read the comments written on their cards. The husband admits that he needs to write things down because otherwise he would never remember them. The wife reports that she put the baby down early four out of the five nights and that she thinks she followed through pretty well on her commitment. She thanks him for the evenings he initiated conversations. He shares that he initiated three talks and that he enjoyed being with her. He says that he can see the benefits of loving her the way God wants him to love her.

This outcome may seem too good to be true, but it's not. It won't happen this way every time, obviously. But if you follow these four steps on even a fairly regular basis, God will speak to you through His Word. You'll be able to help each other apply it, and God will bless you.

# 15

# SPIRITUAL
# CONVERSATIONS

*Making God Part of Your Daily Dialogue*

*I*t's Memorial Day weekend, and you're preparing to line up with thirty-two other drivers for the start of the most important auto race in the world—the Indianapolis 500. You are surrounded by finely tuned, high-performance racecars. You marvel at all these sleek, aerodynamic machines with huge tires and massive horsepower. They are, without question, the fastest track cars ever built.

Your vehicle? You are behind the wheel of a go-cart with a lawn mower engine. What's worse, you don't seem to realize that you have a problem.

Sitting in your go-cart in pit row, you gun your three horsepower engine a few times and look around, hoping to get some impressed looks from the other drivers. What you get are a number of amused glances and some outright belly laughs. *Wait until we're out on the track, fancy boys,* you think. *You'll be choking on my fumes.*

An older, white-haired gentleman comes up to you and makes you a surprising offer. He says that he'll let you drive his

Indy car. He says that it's the most powerful and dependable car ever made. And that's not all. The distinguished-looking man tells you that he's no Johnny-come-lately to the racing business. He has been involved in car racing for fifty years and knows all there is to know about engines, tires, and race strategy. His teams have won many championship trophies.

He volunteers his services to you. He'll be on your team. He'll guide you during the race from the pit area. He tells you that he's offering you the chance of a lifetime.

Drumming your fingers on your small, rubber steering wheel, you consider his offer for several minutes. Then you say, "No, thanks. I won't need your help. I'll stick to my own mean machine."

What chance would you have to win the race? Zero. What chance do you have even to survive the race? Slim.

You might not realize it, but I've just described the situation in most marriages. Like you in the go-cart, most couples are failing to take advantage of something that will lead to real success in their relationship. Without this critical ingredient, you have exactly the same chance of building a great marriage as you do of winning the Indy 500 in your putt-putt cart—zero.

Like the old man in my story, I am offering you something that will help you win and win big in your marriage. (It's my story, so I can cast myself as the hero). This something is *spiritual conversations*. If you and your spouse will talk about God and spiritual matters regularly, you will achieve a deeper level of intimacy. You will feel God's presence, and you will spiritually bond. You will win the marriage race.

## CREATE THE KOINONIA

The Greek term used in the New Testament to describe true fellowship is *koinonia* (1 Corinthians 10:16; Philemon 1:6). It refers to the unique bond shared only by Christians. Indeed, the closest relationships are among Christians. Why? Because what we have in common is Jesus Christ and our love for Him. Jesus is the foundation of our relationships. *Koinonia* is the developing of intimate relationships with other followers of Jesus through communicating on the spiritual level.

I believe strongly that you can have *koinonia* as a Christian couple. So many couples communicate only on a superficial level—they talk only about the kids, the house, business matters, sports, food, friends, family, current events, and the weather. It's easy to talk about these safe, nonthreatening topics, but it doesn't do much for your intimacy. ("Wow, honey! Talking about Jimmy's chicken pox and the leaky roof makes me feel tingly all over and very close to you.")

If you want real depth in your marriage, you need to learn to talk with each other spiritually. When I tell Sandy how God is working in my life, I open a door so she can see inside me. When I share with her how I'm doing in my relationship with Jesus, she really knows me at the core of my being. Because Jesus is the center of my life, I'm sharing the most important and personal part of me.

Admittedly, communicating with your spouse spiritually does not come naturally. Just as with prayers, Bible reading and study, and other spiritual bonding activities, you need to learn how to create spiritual conversations. Your conversations about spiritual matters will take place on three different levels. Let's look at them.

## 1. The Personal Level

You learn to tell your partner, regularly and in detail, about your spiritual life: what you're doing in your daily quiet time with God, insights you've gained in your Bible reading, and how you're applying the Bible to your life. You need to talk about your spiritual victories—those times when God gave you the power to share Christ with a coworker, overcome a weakness, or help a friend in need. You also need to admit your spiritual defeats—those times when you failed to obey God, read your Bible regularly, or impact those around you for Christ. When Satan attacks you—and he will—tell your partner and pray about it together.

Each of you can share how God is working in your individual lives and how He is using daily events to guide and teach you. People frequently say to me, "Dave, I just live life, and things happen. I know God is in charge, but He's not really all that involved in the details of my life, is He?" I reply: "Oh, yes, He is—if you know Him."

Once you have a relationship with God through Jesus, He is with you twenty-four hours a day. He's guiding and leading you. He's creating events every day to teach you, to develop your character, and to build your faith in Him. God is choreographing your entire life! Once you open your eyes and see what He's doing, your whole perspective changes. No day is ever again routine because your sovereign God is the director of every scene, every event, every interaction.

This is not only good for your personal spiritual life, but it also provides an inexhaustible supply of conversational material for you and your spouse. You can come home every day and say, "Guess what God did in my life today!"

In fact, He made lots of things happen in your day. All for you! When you start noticing God's involvement in your day, you'll have things to talk about. You'll have some terrific conversations that are personal, revealing, stimulating, and encouraging.

## 2. *The Relationship Level*

You can also talk about how God is working in your marriage. He is intimately involved in the details of your relationship. About once or twice a month, you need to ask each other some searching spiritual questions. What is God teaching us lately as a couple? What does God want us to learn from each other? How is He guiding us through painful areas of our relationship? What good, positive things can we thank Him for? Are we pleasing Him in our marriage?

What you're doing is evaluating your marriage from a spiritual perspective. At its core, your marriage is a spiritual relationship, and God uses events in it to build your faith—to mold your marriage into a dynamic one-flesh relationship that shows the world that God is alive and well.

Do you know there are couples who go days, weeks, months, and even years without ever talking about how God is working in their lives and marriages? Of course you do. Perhaps you've never done this kind of sharing yourselves. Most couples don't because they don't know how spiritual conversations will benefit their marriage.

### 3. The External Level

At this level, you share concerns about other people: family, pastors, friends, coworkers, neighbors, missionaries, people in the news, and political leaders. You dialogue about the physical health, relationship problems, and spiritual health of people you care about. You talk about what you can learn from the lives of others—from their mistakes, their hardships, or their steps of faith. There are valuable lessons to be learned from watching and talking about the lives of Christians and non-Christians around you.

## GETTING A MAN TO TALK ABOUT SPIRITUAL MATTERS

Let's be honest. It's easy to explain these three levels of spiritual conversation, but it's tough to actually do them. I can hear the women readers: "He won't talk to me about his trip to the hardware store! How can I get him to talk about spiritual things?" I have some strategies that will help.

Because of our male-female differences, regular conversations between spouses can be difficult. As with all other areas of life, men and women approach spiritual issues quite differently. Spiritual conversations are even more difficult because they require more openness and vulnerability. Frankly, most husbands aren't known for those traits. Most men initially respond to God and spiritual events with logic. They rationalize. They focus on the facts. They plan a course of action. They *think* first. Conversely, most women initially respond with emotion. They go with their instincts, their gut reactions, their intuition. They *feel* first.

Men need time and space to process spiritual issues. They respond more slowly to questions of faith. Women respond to God and His truth more quickly. Rick Chappell, a friend and pastor, says women use the "Pentium E"—emotions—to process spiritual truth. While the man uses a paper and pencil to figure out how God wants him to respond, the woman hits a few computer keys and prints out a response in a flash.

Men are less verbal about faith than women. This shouldn't come as a shock to you women, since men are less verbal than you about almost everything. It's tough—extremely tough—for a man to talk spiritually with his wife. But he can learn how, and you can help him by following some basic communication principles.

## A Few Tips for Women

Ladies, start with prayer. Even if you both pray silently, or you pray out loud and he doesn't, the act of talking to God is an effective way to warm up for a spiritual conversation. Prayer puts the man in a spiritual mood and makes him aware of God's presence.

Before you begin to talk, ask the man to listen to you and respond to what you say. Tell him you really need his attention and his reaction. Tell him that by being a good sounding board, he'll help you grow spiritually. Most men don't naturally like to talk, but they do like to feel needed. If he does a decent job of listening and providing a few responses, he'll connect with you spiritually and be drawn into the conversation.

You'll have to teach him gently how to reflect what you're saying and feeling. Ask him to repeat key words and phrases you use. Ask him to identify your emotions and to try to feel just a little bit of what you're feeling. If you're confused, you want him to feel your confusion. If you're angry, he can be angry along with you. If you're happy, he can be happy along with you. Stop every so often and ask him, "What do you think I'm feeling right now?" Tell him that by interacting with you in this way, you'll know that he's listening and you won't have to keep talking and repeating yourself. Believe me, that will motivate him to work on these skills.

Another thing, ladies: be *brief*. Speak for two or three minutes. Then be quiet. Do not rattle on and on, hoping that your volume of words will increase the chances of a response. All it will do is increase your chances of his brain shutting down. Especially in a spiritual conversation, less is more. Make a few comments, and then give him a chance to respond.

If he responds with logic, which he's likely to do, interrupt him by saying: "Honey, that's logic. I need listening and understanding, okay?" If you don't cut in and get him back on track, the conversation won't go anywhere. You'll feel hurt, resentful, and completely misunderstood. He's not being malicious with his logic. In fact, he thinks he's doing a public service when he says something like: "Sweetheart, you're just too upset about this. God is a loving God, and it doesn't help to doubt Him. Just let it go and everything will work out just fine." Statements like these are not a public service; they are a public nuisance. Thank him for trying to help, but tell him that you want him to get back in the listening mode.

After you've spoken to him about spiritual matters for a few minutes, it's okay to ask him a few questions and bring up a few issues you'd like him to comment on. It's the *way* you ask him to respond that's important. Use words like these: "Honey, you don't have to respond right now [he wasn't going to anyway, but this relieves any pressure he might be feeling]. When you're ready, I'd like to hear what your reaction is to what I said." It's essential to use the words *when you're ready* with a man because he needs to feel in control. He must respond in his time and on his terms. You've given him that manly right, and he'll appreciate it. It doesn't guarantee a response, but it increases the odds.

A man needs time to process what you've said and figure out how to react. He quite literally cannot respond to you right away. He's not made that way. He can listen and provide a few under-standing, reflective responses to what you said, but he has to think about and organize any kind of a deeper, meaningful response. He must pull away and sort out his own internal thoughts and feelings.

It might take him twenty minutes, two hours, or two days to process your comments and formulate his reaction. Ladies, you must give the man this time. I call it "riding the train." He'll jump on the train, do his processing, and then ride the train back to you. Only then will he start sharing what he's found out.

If he's riding the train and you see no sign of him returning, do not nag. No man ever responded well to nagging. I think it's rea-sonable for you to remind him *one time* about the issue. Say, "Remember that topic I brought up two days ago? When you're ready, I'd like to hear your comments about it. I'm very interested in your thoughts." After this one prompt, let it go. He obviously won't ride the train and return to talk about every spiritual subject you bring up. If these communication tips lead him to return 20 or 30 percent of the time, that'll be way above the national average.

It's critical to realize that you and your husband will only begin to talk on a deeper spiritual level in stages. No married couple can learn to engage in deep, intimate conversation—spiri-tual or otherwise—in one sitting. By following these suggestions, you can extend your conversations and go deeper and deeper as you progress.

The best conversations occur over two, three, or four days, as you keep revisiting the same topics. The woman brings up a spiritual issue, and the man listens and reflects. He rides the train to process, then returns and restarts the conversation with his response. The woman reacts to what he says, and then he rides the train again. It will typically take four or five train trips before the man gets deep and really expresses his personal, spiritual reaction. (For more on this communication technique, see my book *Men Are Clams, Women Are Crowbars*.)

Here's one last idea that will help men begin spiritual conversations with their wives. I call it "the Pad." Most Christian men do have spiritual insights, ideas, and feelings during the day. They do see God working in their lives. The problem is that by the end of the day they can't remember their spiritual experiences. The day will have become one big blank.

## A FEW TIPS FOR MEN

Men, don't trust your memory. Do what I do—buy several notepads, attach pens to them, and keep them in strategic places. Throughout the day as you notice the hand of God in your life, jot down these spiritual events on your pad. That night, or the next time you and your wife meet to have your spiritual talk, you'll have a list of things to say. Your wife will be thrilled. God will be pleased.

As I write these words, my day is winding down. Check out this brief list of God-inspired events that I wrote down on my pad:

1. God used me to help a young man achieve a break-through in therapy. He's going to deal directly with his parents and express the pain they've caused him.

2. A dynamic local church in which I've being trying to get the opportunity to speak called today and scheduled a speaking engagement. God opened the door!

3. My secretary, Ethel, is struggling because it's the first anniversary of the death of her dear husband, Ed. We

talked for a while. God showed me how precious Sandy is to me and the need to cherish every moment together. God also used Ethel to show me real faith and spiritual maturity in action.

When Sandy and I sit down tomorrow evening to talk, I'll share these items. Sandy will be impressed. More important, we'll have an opportunity to spiritually bond.

Being intentional about your conversations can take you and your spouse to a deeper level of spiritual intimacy. Deliberately and purposefully making God a part of your daily dialogue will propel you far above the level of mediocrity.

# GIVE GOD THE GLORY

*The Wonders of Worshiping Together*

ave you seen *Antiques Roadshow,* the phenomenally successful PBS television series? Sandy and our three girls love that show. They get their hot tea and popcorn and settle in on the couch for each thrilling episode. The show travels from city to city with a group of professional appraisers from leading auction houses and antique companies. In every city people line up by the thousands, bringing their antiques to find out what they're worth. Each half hour program contains the thirty or so best stories about the antiques.

Frankly, I fail to see the attraction of this show. I just don't get it. People drag in a hodgepodge of sorry-looking old stuff to be appraised: jewelry, vases, lamps, dolls, furniture, toys, photographs. It looks like a televised garage sale to me.

The expert appraisers seem to revel in their ability to reel off a mind-boggling list of obscure, complicated details about these antiques. "Yes, Madam, this bureau was made in the spring of 1736 by a man who had the beginning stages of Parkinson's disease. You can see that a slightly shaking hand made these marks.

These ridges here symbolize the Hawthorne Mountain Range of Eastern Austria. This was one of only 249 such pieces made by the Arthur Fattenbury Company." How could anyone know so much minutiae about such dusty-musty articles?

Just once, I want the appraiser to say: "Really, my dear lady, who do you think you're kidding, bringing this piece to me? You've kept this...this...*thing* for forty years for nothing. You're wasting my time. Anyone can see that it's worthless. The only possible use for it would be as a paperweight. It looks to me like early 1960s K-Mart. It's worth fifty cents, tops. My suggestion: Drop it in that garbage can on your way out."

This never happens, of course. The antiques being appraised are almost always worth far more than anyone would ever dream. Even though I've been poking fun at *Antiques Roadshow,* the truth is there are real, honest-to-goodness treasures unearthed on this show. Some of the plain-looking, completely unexciting items turn out to be incredibly valuable.

On one show, an older woman brought a small card table to be appraised. It looked ordinary and unimpressive. The woman obviously didn't expect it to be worth much. She just wanted to know the history of the table, which had been in her family for years. She—along with my family watching the show—was shocked when the appraiser told her that she had a rare eighteenth-century card table worth a small fortune. Purchased at a garage sale for twenty-five dollars, it sold for *five hundred thousand dollars* at Sotheby's, the famous auction house in New York City. Wow! I haven't made fun of this show since.

It just goes to show you that treasures can be found in unlikely places. In fact, I'm here to tell you that you have a valuable treasure in your home, though you may not have discovered it yet. No, I don't mean an old lamp or antique chest of drawers up in the attic.

I'm talking about worship. Worshiping together as a couple is a treasure of spiritual intimacy that few couples find in their marriages. With a little bit of guidance and instruction, you can have the priceless experience of worship over and over again.

## WHY WE WORSHIP

We are made to worship God. It is our highest purpose in life. A. W. Tozer put it simply and eloquently: "God is trying to call us back to that for which He created us, to worship Him and enjoy Him forever."[1]

We are commanded to worship God (Deuteronomy 6:13; 1 Chronicles 16:29; Matthew 4:10), but worship is also the natural response to a God who has given us too many blessings to count. We worship God because it delights and pleases Him (Psalm 104:34; 149:4–5) and because it draws us closer to Him (Psalm 99:5; 132:7; 145:18).

We also worship God because it draws us closer to our marriage partners. In the powerful mixture of reverence, awe, and joy that is worship, there is a God-given spiritual intimacy we can't get anywhere else. We are never closer to God than when we are worshiping Him. And we are never closer to each other than when we are worshiping God *together.*

## PUBLIC WORSHIP

The church I belong to, Christ Community Church in Tampa, Florida, is an exciting place to be during our praise and worship time on Sunday mornings. We've got the choir. We've got chorus leaders. We've got the band and all the instruments—keyboard, guitar, bass, drums, trumpet, trombone, and saxophone. We've got Michael Dawson, who is James Brown, the Temptations, Nat King Cole, and the Pips all rolled into one fabulous voice.

When we sing the choruses, we have about as much fun as Christians can have here on earth. The music is pumping, and the congregation is standing. Michael is doing his thing; everybody is praising God with their voices and swaying to the music... and Sandy and I are worshiping God side by side, surrounded by our friends and fellow believers in Christ. Our hearts fill with love for our heavenly Father. We thoroughly enjoy it, and we know that God thoroughly enjoys it.

God wants us to worship Him publicly (Hebrews 10:25). The Israelites did, according to the Old Testament. The early church did, according to the New Testament. It's important—to God and to your marriage—to sit together during church services and worship. I often come across couples who don't attend worship services together on a regular basis. These poor souls are usually overcommitted and have church responsibilities that prevent them from worshiping together. (Of course, many people are so busy that they skip church altogether.)

I say *poor souls* because these couples are cheating themselves out of a marriage-enriching experience. They're also cheating God out of worship that He is entitled to and worthy to receive. If you must miss the Sunday morning service, make every effort to go to another worship service—Sunday evening, Wednesday evening—during the week.

## PRIVATE WORSHIP

As important as public worship is, there is another type of worship that is even more spiritually beneficial to your marriage. You find the real treasure of worship when you and your spouse worship privately together in a quiet place in your home with no distractions.

Let's take a look at one couple's private worship time. I'll call this couple Mark and Sharon. They've been developing their spiritual intimacy for some time, so their worship is at a more advanced stage. It's Sunday evening, and Mark reminds Sharon that it's time for their monthly worship. After making sure the children understand that they need to stay in their rooms for the next thirty minutes, this couple sits down on the couch in the den. Holding hands, they praise God in conversational prayer. They go back and forth, thanking God for all He's done for them, their marriage, their family, and their friends.

A few minutes into the praise time, Mark gets up and puts on a compact disc of praise choruses. They sing together softly with their eyes closed, thinking about the words. It's unlikely that either one would ever be asked to sing in church, but they don't care. And neither does God. They have worked through their initial awkwardness and embarrassment and now enjoy praising God through their private duets.

Mark and Sharon find plenty of scriptural support for their singing. As Paul wrote to the believers at Ephesus:

> Do not get drunk with wine, for that is dissipation, but be filled with the Spirit, speaking to one another in psalms and hymns and spiritual songs, singing and making melody with your heart to the Lord. (Ephesians 5:18–19)

After a few minutes of singing, Mark and Sharon move into a time of adoration of God and Jesus Christ in prayer. With the music still playing in the background, they praise and glorify God for His attributes—His patience, love, grace, loving-kindness, sovereignty, and omniscience.

They adore Jesus Christ, following Paul's teaching:

> Therefore also God highly exalted Him, and bestowed on Him the name which is above every name, that at the name of Jesus every knee should bow, of those who are in heaven, and on earth, and under the earth, and that every tongue should confess that Jesus Christ is Lord, to the glory of God the Father. (Philippians 2:9–11)

They continue praying, mentioning personal concerns and the needs of others. They bring up areas of their relationship that they need God's help to improve. There are periods of silence during which they reflect, meditate, or just rest together in the presence of their loving Father and Savior. Mark and Sharon have discovered that they don't need to worry about following a strict, planned-out schedule. The Holy Spirit guides and directs the process.

Although it doesn't happen tonight, Mark and Sharon sometimes include other activities in their worship time. They may read a passage of Scripture, usually a psalm, and meditate on it. They like the Psalms because they're filled with praises and the language of worship. They may read from a devotional book. About once every three months, they have a private communion service with bread and grape juice.

Tonight's worship time lasted only twenty minutes. Some worship times are shorter, and some are longer. It depends on their schedule and how the Spirit leads. Mark and Sharon feel good about worshiping God and enjoy the unique closeness it gives them as a couple. They've also found that the spiritual togetherness their worship produces lasts for several days. It lingers and has a positive impact on other areas of their relationship.

Can you picture you and your spouse having private worship times like Mark and Sharon? It takes courage, vulnerability, and practice to worship like this. You'll have to push past all your excuses, defenses, and feelings of awkwardness. I urge you to try it. Once you've experienced worship together, you'll want to keep it up. You'll realize that you're doing something that God created you to do—something that will add a whole new and exciting dimension to your spiritual bond.

Best of all, God will use worship to change you and mold you into who He wants you to be. Warren Wiersbe, a well-known author and theologian, made this point in his classic book *Real Worship:*

It is this kind of experience to which you and I are called by God. He wants to transform us. He also wants to work through us to transform the people and circumstances that make up our lives. Every Christian is either a "conformer" or a "transformer." We are either fashioning our lives by pressure from without, or we are transforming our lives by power from within. The difference is—worship.[2]

Do you want to transform your personal life? Then worship God on your own. Do you want to transform your marriage? Then worship God as a couple.

1. A. W. Tozer, *What Ever Happened to Worship?* (Camp Hill, Pa.: Christian Publications, 1985), 12.

2. Warren W. Wiersbe, *Real Worship* (Nashville, Tenn.: Oliver Nelson, 1986), 31.

# DISCIPLESHIP IN MARRIAGE

*Keeping Each Other Accountable*

I've always loved team sports, especially soccer and baseball. Looking back over my athletic career and all the teams I played on, I remember every coach very clearly. I had all kinds of coaches—short, tall, fat, skinny, nice, mean, gracious, and spiteful. Some were Christians and some were not. Although every one of them impacted my life, two stand out in my mind: my first coach and my last coach.

My first coach was a kind man and a tremendous encourager. When I showed up at the first day of practice for the Dodgers, a Little League baseball team, I was scared to death. I'd never played on a real team before. The coach came over, shook my hand, and made me feel right at home. He didn't rant and rave and scream at his players the way some Little League coaches do. He wanted us to learn how to play baseball and have fun. For him, winning was secondary.

It was a good thing that the coach didn't care about winning, because our team was lousy. A lot of us were new to the game, and our skills were largely undeveloped. Not many of the guys could throw the ball accurately, so my coach had trouble finding a pitcher. To my surprise, he chose me! I didn't have blinding speed with my fastball, but I could get the ball over the plate.

Three-quarters of the way through our first season, the Dodgers were firmly entrenched in last place. We had lost almost every game. Even though I was the losing pitcher in all those games, the coach stuck with me. He kept saying: "David, you're doing a good job. You can do it, son." I kept pitching, and I kept getting hammered. Of course, it would have helped if the guys behind me could have caught a few balls and made some plays.

Then came the big game. We had to play the best team in the league. I forget the name of that team, but they wore dark green uniforms, and they were big. Those kids were giants! They were cocky, and they laughed at us from their dugout. They knew that they were going to win.

But that night the craziest thing happened. They didn't win. We won! Those overdeveloped, mutant, juvenile delinquents couldn't hit my pitches. I mowed down hitter after hitter, just like Nolan Ryan. When they did hit the ball, my teammates caught it! It was like the movie *Angels in the Outfield*, in which angels help a hapless team go all the way to the World Series. After the final out, my coach gave me a big hug and said: "See? I knew you could do it."

Then there was my last coach, the soccer coach at Point Loma College in San Diego. Off the field, he was a great guy—friendly, funny, and caring. On the field, he was Vince Lombardi—intense, tough as nails, and driven to succeed. Coach's hallmark was his focus on conditioning. We were just a small Christian college, but we had to play some huge universities like San Diego State. The first day of practice, Coach told us that we were inferior to these teams in terms of our ability and experience but that we would make up for these liabilities with superb conditioning.

We looked at each other and asked with trepidation, "What does

Coach mean by superb conditioning?" We found out that he meant "the sand hill." We practiced on a field set in a bowl with huge hills on two sides. On one hill, there was a large sandy area. Every day after practice, Coach said, "It's time for the sand hill, boys." He called us *boys* because we weren't men until we survived the hill.

With Coach standing at the bottom, we sprinted single file up and down that hill. Forty yards up and forty yards down. Over and over and over. Our feet would dig into the soft sand, making every step an effort. Guys would collapse, throw up, lose their balance, fall, and cry for their mamas. But Mama wasn't there—just Coach. Finally, when we felt as though we'd die if we had to take another step on that horrible hill, Coach said, "All right, *men,* hit the showers."

As much as I despised that coach for forcing me to run that sand hill, as the season wore on I realized that his conditioning program paid off. As a team, we were in great shape. We could run and run and not get winded. As an individual, I learned that I could get through anything by just sticking with it. Coach taught me how to develop self-discipline, courage, and stamina. He taught me never to quit and always to give my best effort. These qualities have served me well—in my spiritual life, in my career, and in my marriage.

What these coaches did was *hold me accountable.* They taught me, encouraged me, confronted me, and pushed me. They made me work hard both on my athletic skills and my character. I gave them the right to drive me and mold me because I knew that they had my best interests at heart.

Accountability is allowing someone else to examine your life in a particular area and to give you direct feedback on how to improve. You let this person call you to account. You invite this person to tell you the truth about you. To make yourself accountable requires a great deal of trust on your part. It requires you to be open and vulnerable. That's risky, but it's worth the risk.

Everybody needs a coach, an accountability partner who

cares enough about you to push you to be your best. Actually, you need more than one accountability partner. Right now, I have a number of people holding me accountable in different areas of my life. At the office, it's my secretary, Ethel Harris. In my therapy practice, it's my dad and Dr. Tim Foster. In the financial area, it's my brother-in-law (and crack CPA) Eric Martin. In my spiritual life, the most important area of all, I have three people who keep me on the right track—my friends Rocky Glisson and Larry Schweizer and my wife, Sandy.

Sandy is my most significant and valuable partner in spiritual accountability because she knows me better than anyone else. While I tell others what's happening in my spiritual life, Sandy *witnesses* what I do. The accountability in our spiritual lives goes both ways: Sandy is also accountable to me.

Our decision to be mutual, spiritual accountability partners has led both Sandy and me to a deeper walk with Jesus Christ. It has led us to take steps to spiritual maturity that we would not have taken alone. It has led to a stronger spiritual bond.

## ACCOUNTABILITY IS A DIRTY WORD

In our society, *accountability* is a dirty, fourteen-letter word. Americans are a fiercely independent people. In American culture, accomplishing great things *on your own* is held up as the ideal. Asking for help shows weakness. Frank Sinatra didn't sing "I Did It by Being Accountable." His classic "I Did It My Way" is the national anthem of the independent, entrepreneurial American style of life.

Nevertheless, without accountability, change and growth are unlikely to occur in your life. If you answer to no one, you don't have to change. No one knows the weak areas you need to work on, and no one comes alongside to force you to face yourself and take steps to grow. Christian clients sometimes say to me, "I don't need to mention this problem to anyone else. I'll just pray to God." I respond, "That's not good enough. Certainly, pray about it often. But also make yourself accountable to someone. If you don't, I doubt that you'll ever overcome it."

What's more, if you have no accountability, you probably won't be close to anyone either. As Mr. or Mrs. Independent, you build walls around you that no one can get through. You may feel safe in there, but it's awfully lonely. If you don't allow another person access to your life—especially your spiritual life—no one can really know you. The people around you—family, friends, coworkers, fellow church members, neighbors—will know only the image you project. That's not the real you! And if others don't know who you really are, they can't love you.

God designed marriage to be the perfect relationship for spiritual accountability. There is tremendous safety and security inside the marriage relationship. When you share the details of your walk with Christ, your spouse won't think less of you. Your spouse won't tell anyone your spiritual secrets. Your spouse will love you and help you heal, grow, and progress spiritually.

## WHAT THE BIBLE SAYS

God wants us to be accountable. The Bible teaches accountability in clear, specific language. The central principle is found in Proverbs 27:17: "Iron sharpens iron, so one man sharpens another." Christians are also instructed to:

- exhort and encourage one another (Hebrews 3:13; 10:24);
- rebuke and confront one another honestly even when it hurts (Proverbs 27:6; Psalm 141:5);
- directly address the sin in a fellow believer's life by following a series of gradually escalating steps as described by Jesus (Matthew 18:15–17).

In addition to specific teaching, the Bible is replete with examples of accountable relationships: Moses and Joshua; Esther and Mordecai; David and Jonathan; Paul and Barnabas; Paul and Timothy. A closer look at these relationships reveals that they involved discipleship. Their ultimate purpose was to help each person in the relationship grow spiritually.

Spiritual growth and maturity in Christ through discipleship is what accountability in marriage is all about. My job is to hold Sandy accountable so that she will have the deepest and best possible relationship with Jesus Christ. Her job is to do the same thing for me. In essence, we disciple each other. There are three main ways we do this:

## 1. Answer the Tough Questions

A vital part of accountability is agreeing to answer to your marriage partner for your spiritual life. You have no secrets. On a routine basis, you sit together in a private place and, eyeball-to-eyeball, ask each other the tough questions:

- Did you have your daily quiet times this week?
- What did you do in your quiet times?
- Which book of the Bible are you reading now?
- Which verse or passage did you apply this week?
- What is God doing in your life?
- Which area of your spiritual life is a struggle?

When I tell couples to ask each other these questions once a week, their jaws usually drop about a foot. They look at me as if I'd lost my mind. They say, "This is like putting our spiritual lives under a microscope!" And I reply, "That's exactly right. But that's the only way you'll change and grow spiritually. The unexamined life—and, therefore, the life without accountability—stays just the way it is."

I ask these couples to study the Gospels to find out how Jesus interacted with His twelve disciples. Talk about accountability! From early morning to late at night, He was on them—

teaching, encouraging, confronting, admonishing. He examined their lives every day and held them to a high standard. And, with the exception of Judas Iscariot, these men were never the same again. They became like Jesus. They changed the world.

Allowing your partner to ask tough questions demands real strength and integrity. It requires that you give up your precious, jealously guarded privacy and natural protectiveness. Many individuals have told me, "Dave, my spiritual life is a private matter. It's my own business. I don't share it with anyone." I tell them, "Of course, you don't open up and share with just anyone. But you need to share it with your spouse—your sweetheart, your lover, your best friend, your life's mate."

## 2. Meet Spiritual Needs

Accountability also means committing to grow spiritually in the ways that you and your partner decide are best for you. You identify weaknesses in your spouse's walk with Christ, and you work together to improve them. These areas of weakness are *spiritual needs*. With the help of your partner, you must confront these spiritual needs to mature in Christ.

Here's how one couple went about meeting a spiritual need. The wife had an ongoing battle with poor self-esteem and lack of assertiveness. She was too nice and would not respond when someone mistreated her. One evening, she told her husband that she had just learned that a good friend at church had gossiped about her. She was deeply hurt and angry. After discussion and prayer, they decided that this was a God-given opportunity to meet the wife's spiritual need in the area of assertiveness.

Her husband told her that if she could "speak the truth in love" (Ephesians 4:15) with this friend, it would be a big step in her struggle to become more assertive. This helped her see that it was not just an emotional issue, but also a spiritual one. Her husband prepared her for the confrontation by role-playing the scene and praying with her about it.

With his support, she did it. She told her friend the truth about gossip and its painful effect on her. Even though her friend did not respond well, she knew she had done the right thing. She let go of her resentment and gave her friend an opportunity to change. When she told her husband what had happened, they had an intimate time of sharing and celebration.

### 3. Set Specific Spiritual Goals

Without goals, you have no clear direction, and you end up treading water spiritually. Recently, I told Sandy that while I was praying, God laid on my heart the need to share the gospel with a certain neighbor in the coming week. You know what Sandy did? She said, "Great, Dave. Let's pray about that right now, and this Saturday at four o'clock in the afternoon I'll ask you how it went."

Whoa! What do you think the chances were that I'd follow through and talk to my neighbor about Jesus? Very high. In fact, just about 100 percent. I knew Sandy wouldn't forget to bring it up. (The woman has never forgotten anything in her life.) I didn't want to face my wife and have to say, "Uh, you know, I didn't get around to…." No way! I wasn't going to look small in my wife's eyes. I was going to be her hero. I was going to be a man of my word. Besides, we would have a great spiritual conversation about what God did as I shared the gospel. I didn't want to miss that either.

I did witness to my neighbor that week. Frankly, it was awkward and didn't go all that well. But I did it, and I felt God's presence with me. Sandy was proud of me, and we did have a great talk about how it went.

## BE CONSISTENT

I recommend that you hold each other accountable once a week in these three areas—answering the tough questions, meeting spiritual needs, and setting specific spiritual goals. Your weekly spiritual evaluation meeting is the perfect time to do this. At a minimum, discuss these accountability issues every two weeks. This kind of regularity keeps you fresh and current. If you know that your partner is going to probe into your spiritual life weekly or biweekly, you'll change. You'll have no choice.

Some of you probably have a friend or mentor who serves as an accountability partner. That's terrific. Keep that one-on-one relationship going. You might also consider finding an older, wiser couple to hold you and your marriage partner accountable. Couples need accountability just as individuals do. Having a mentor couple who will ask the difficult questions, provide teaching and advice, and keep you on the spiritual bonding path is a tremendous asset to your marriage.

Whatever you do, I urge you to use your spouse as your main accountability partner. It will make you both stronger spiritually. It will draw you closer spiritually. Like Jesus' disciples, you will never be the same. A nice bonus is that your marriage will never be the same either.

# 18

# TEAMWORK FOR THE KINGDOM

❧

*Serving Side by Side*

What's it like serving God together—as a couple? What are the benefits of teaming up to have a spiritual impact on others? Is it really worth the time, effort, and inconvenience? You'll find the answers to these questions in the stories of two couples.

The first couple, Mike and Gloria, had pretty much everything the world had to offer. Mike had an extremely good job. They had a nice home, two new cars, and a couple of healthy kids. They were living the American dream. They both were Christians and faithfully attended a local, Bible-believing church.

But all was not perfect in paradise. Far from it. Mike and Gloria had an ingrained pattern of bickering. They squabbled frequently and kept up a steady stream of snide, critical comments. Their inability to resolve conflicts was taking a toll on their relationship. They weren't having fun anymore. Romance was practically nonexistent, and sex was boring. Spiritually, they had no passion. They went to church but didn't get much out of it. They were not happy but didn't know what to do about it.

Gloria made the first move to change things. She went to a women's conference and came back convicted of the need to get involved in evangelism. She shared with Mike her burden to bring others to Christ and asked him to consider joining her in this new endeavor. Over the course of two weeks, they discussed it and prayed about it. Then they acted.

They joined a ministry team that called on non-Christian married couples and singles who were new to the church. Every Wednesday evening, they called on these people together. They built relationships and led others to Christ. But Mike and Gloria didn't stop there. They also reached out to unsaved neighbors and started conversations about Jesus Christ. They began a weekly Bible study for spiritual seekers in their home. When they led others to Christ, they followed up with several months of discipleship. They couldn't believe how much fun it was bringing people into the kingdom of God.

Mike and Gloria's service for Christ changed their spiritual lives. They were once again excited about their Christian faith and grew by leaps and bounds—individually and as a couple. Their service also changed their marriage. They developed a level of camaraderie and friendship that they hadn't had for years. In fact, they had never been so close. They stopped their continual bickering. The joy of bringing others to Christ—together—helped them put the love and intimacy back into their marriage.

The second couple, Bob and Susie, also needed something to get their marriage back on track. Their communication had been poor for years. They just couldn't seem to connect on a deep level. All they talked about was the house, their jobs, and the kids. Bob was a stick—unemotional, rational, unreachable. He didn't like to listen to a woman talk and share a bunch of feelings and details. Unfortunately for Bob, that's what Susie does (and most women do) in conversation. Susie wanted closeness with Bob but couldn't get him to open up.

There were also some serious sexual problems in the marriage. Their lack of emotional intimacy led to stale, infrequent sex. A huge part of the problem was Bob's addiction to pornography. He had rented X-rated movies for years and recently had begun using the Internet late at night to feed his lust. When Susie found out what he was doing, she was disgusted and deeply hurt.

Bob and Susie attended church and served regularly in their own individual areas. But they had never served God together. That all changed one night when their pastor asked them to temporarily fill a slot on the junior high ministry team. They reluctantly agreed, making it clear that they would stay only for a month or two. It's been five years now, and they're still on the team.

Bob and Susie fell in love with the junior high kids. They opened their home for youth group Bible studies, parties, and for anybody who had a problem and needed to talk. They taught these kids. They played and prayed with them. They even led a group of twenty-five youth on a short-term mission trip to Mexico. On the trip, God gave them a taste of His awesome power and incredible grace. They saw villagers hungry for the love of Jesus. They saw great poverty and great needs. They saw miracles. They saw God produce new spiritual maturity in the kids' lives and in their own lives.

Bob and Susie fell in love with Jesus again, and they fell in love with each other again. They expected to teach the group members a few things about God, life, and relationships. Instead, God used the group to teach Bob and Susie many things. Serving together forced them to talk about deeper issues: the kids, ministry plans, and God's desires for the youth group. They prayed together often—for the strength to keep serving, for the individual kids and their needs, and for God to make clear what He wanted them to learn from the experience.

Their service helped Bob and Susie break through the barriers that blocked their communication. Bob began to open up and share his personal thoughts and feelings. His closer walk with

Jesus gave him the confidence and power to address his addiction to pornography. He went to counseling, joined a sexual addiction group, and made real progress in defeating this problem. Susie warmed up and began to respond to Bob with a kind of love and gentleness she hadn't shown in years. They both said that their marriage was more intimate and enjoyable than it ever had been.

## TEAM UP FOR CHRIST

These are true stories about real people. I know these two couples personally. They have three things in common. First, they're serving Jesus Christ together. Second, they have strong, vibrant spiritual bonds. Third, they have dynamic, growing marriages. The passion they have for serving the Lord flows into their marriages. I have learned a valuable lesson from watching their lives: You reap amazing benefits when you team up as a couple for Christ.

I could tell you stories of dozens of couples who have teamed up in dedicated Christian service. As I travel for my speaking ministry, I have the privilege of meeting married couples serving in a wide variety of ministries. These spouses are on fire for Jesus, and it shows. You can see it in their eyes and hear it in the way they talk. These folks are on to something—something big. It's something that all of us need in our marriages.

Serving God together as a team brings you closer spiritually in a unique way. Consider Aquila and Priscilla, that dynamic duo in the early church. There are several references in the New Testament to their helpfulness and the impressive things they did in service to Christ:

- They took Paul into their home in Corinth. They worked with him in the tent-making trade (Acts 18:2–3).
- They accompanied Paul on a missionary journey to Ephesus (Acts 18:18).
- They took Apollos, a gifted speaker and teacher of the Old Testament, into their home in Ephesus to help him better

understand the things of God (Acts 18:24–26).

✦ Paul described them as "my fellow workers in Christ Jesus" (Romans 16:3).

✦ They risked their lives for Paul, and he and all the Gentile churches were grateful to them (Romans 16:4).

✦ They had a church in their home (1 Corinthians 16:19).

Aquila and Priscilla were sold out to Jesus Christ. They walked alongside Paul (literally and figuratively) and supported his ministry. It's no coincidence that they are always mentioned together in Scripture. What an effective team!

## PICK A PLACE TO SERVE AND JUMP IN

One of the best places to serve God is the local church. The church is God's chosen vehicle to change the world. It's not so important what you do as long as you do *something* together. There are many different areas of service in the church: nursery, teaching Sunday school (elementary, youth, adult), evangelism, discipleship, visitation, music, greeters, mentoring, and so on. Talk to your pastor, pray about it, ask some friends where they think you two could be effective…and then go for it.

There are also many excellent parachurch and community-based ministries: Campus Crusade for Christ, the Navigators, Promise Keepers, Family Life Conferences, Prison Fellowship Ministries, Young Life, homeless shelters, and crisis pregnancy centers. Going on a short-term mission trip is another way to spiritually energize your marriage.

Sandy and I have teamed up in a number of ministry areas throughout our married life. For example, we taught first and second graders at our church for years. (Okay, Sandy taught. I handled crowd control and participated in the activities. But we were still involved *together*.) Those years we spent leading the Sunday school classes helped us build a strong and intimate marital foundation.

Together, we saw God answer many prayer requests for the kids. We saw boys and girls learn about the Bible and how to love Jesus more. We found out about problems occurring in families, and we were able to provide practical help. I remember a number of children who faced serious problems in their homes: no dad present, parents divorcing, an alcoholic parent, a mom or dad with a life-threatening illness. God used Sandy and me to make a difference in the lives of these troubled kids and their families.

It has been exciting to watch the little kids we had in our class grow into young adults. It does make me feel old when one of our former students says, "Wow, Dr. Clarke, is that you? You used to be so...so...young. What happened?" But it's still a thrill to know that God used us as a couple to influence lives for Christ.

Since Sandy and I have four children of our own, we can't serve God together as much as we used to or as much as we wish we could. But we try to join in ministry at least once a year. It may be for a one-time special project. It may be to chaperone the youth group on a few outings. It may be to teach Sunday school or serve in the nursery for a couple of months. We gladly offer what time and energy we have, knowing that we're serving the Lord *and* contributing to the spiritual intimacy of our marriage.

## Enhancing Each Other's Gifts

Serving as a couple does not take the place of serving God as individuals. You can and should do both. In fact, an integral part of your teamwork is to support each other in the application of your spiritual gifts. Help your partner find his spiritual gift. Encourage him to use his gift. Then talk about what God accomplishes through him as he ministers to others with that gift. Let me tell you, these kinds of conversations will be among the best you'll ever have.

Sandy is a skilled administrator. She is organized, hard working, and efficient. She also has a gift for working with kids. She's currently leading a Pioneer Girls club for fifth-grade girls, and she is also involved as a counselor in the Pioneer camping program. My main gift is teaching and communicating God's Word in the practical areas of marriage, parenting, and emotional health. I maintain my counseling practice, present seminars, teach seminary classes, and write books. When asked, I serve as a teacher in Sunday school classes.

Even though we serve God separately in these areas, Sandy and I are still a team in the use of our gifts. We help each other find places to plug in and use our gifts. We pray for each other before and during ministry events. We give each other feedback on the development of our gifts. We tell each other when we think that overcommitment is a problem. One of the real joys in our relationship is sharing what God is doing in our separate ministries. I'm proud of Sandy and excited about her work for Jesus Christ. I love hearing her talk about it. I love praising God with her for the incredible things He does through her. And she feels the same way about my ministries.

## BE A GREAT COMMISSION COUPLE

The Bible doesn't beat around the bush when it comes to the importance of service in the Christian life. Read what Paul writes in 2 Corinthians 5:15: "[Christ] died for all, that they who live should no longer live for themselves, but for Him who died and rose again on their behalf."

I love that verse! It doesn't take a scholar or seminary graduate to figure out what it means. We who know Christ are not to live for our own selfish interests. We are to live for Christ. We exist to serve Jesus Christ. That's the essence of life. To a great degree, it's also the essence of marriage.

The final words that Jesus spoke on earth command us to serve:

> Go therefore and make disciples of all the nations, baptizing them in the name of the Father and the Son and

the Holy Spirit, teaching them to observe all that I commanded you; and lo, I am with you always, even to the end of the age. (Matthew 28:19–20)

When we as couples take the great commission seriously, we are sure to reap blessings. Every married couple I talk to who serves Christ together tells me that it brings them closer in a way that words can't describe. Being more intimate isn't the main reason you should team up in ministry. You do it primarily to obey the Bible and please God. But a wonderful by-product is a new depth and closeness in your marriage.

# 19

# BUILDING INTIMACY
# THROUGH ADVERSITY

*Tough Times Can Strengthen Your Marriage*

teve and Debbie walked down the hallway, entered my office for the first time, took their seats on my couch, and told me their story. It was an ugly story—a very ugly story. Their trouble had started six years earlier when Debbie gave birth to a baby boy with health problems. It was every parent's nightmare. Something was wrong with their precious little guy, but no one could tell them what his problem was. Their first child was perfectly healthy. As Christians, they asked God to help the doctors find out what was happening.

The answer they got was not what they wanted to hear. When he was finally diagnosed as autistic, it was a crushing blow. After the first few weeks, Debbie's feelings of shock, denial, and devastation passed, and she began to address the issue. She gathered all the information on autism she could get her hands on. She made countless calls to medical and psychological professionals in an attempt to find the best possible treatment for her son. All the specialists told her that it was critical that both parents be involved in the treatment process. Unfortunately, Steve refused to help.

Steve could not face the reality of living with an autistic son. He had dreamed for years of having a son—a son to take fishing and hunting, to wrestle with on the floor, to play ball with in the yard. He had always envisioned a son who was healthy, energetic, and dexterous. What he got was a son who couldn't talk, couldn't coordinate his movements, and alternated unpredictably from total withdrawal to fits of uncontrollable rage.

Steve withdrew from his son and his wife. He threw himself into his job and stayed away from home as much as he could. As Debbie went from doctor to doctor and program to program, Steve removed himself from the whole process. Debbie was completely on her own, caring for her son and their other child. She tried again and again to get Steve to help, but he ignored her. She was deeply hurt and resentful. They pulled further and further apart. They stopped talking; they stopped making love; they stopped going to church. Their marriage was dying.

The final straw for Debbie was when she discovered that Steve had had two affairs. One had been with her best friend. It was too much for Debbie. She ranted and raved. She wanted out. Lonely and vulnerable, she did something she thought she would never do—she had her own affair.

As they told me their story, I sat there thinking, *This is pretty bad. In fact, this is one of the worst cases I've ever seen. I wonder why these two persons even came in today.* I had no sooner thought this than Debbie said something like, "Pretty bad, huh? I'll bet this is one of the worst cases you've ever heard. You're probably wondering what we're doing here in your office. Well, let me tell you what happened last Sunday."

Debbie and Steve told me that until the previous Sunday morning, they had been ready to divorce. Debbie had seen an attorney, and the papers were about to be filed. Steve wasn't going to fight for the marriage. He wanted a divorce as quickly as possible. But on Sunday morning, out of the clear blue, Steve asked her to go to church. They hadn't been to church for months! Debbie agreed.

Incredibly, Steve and Debbie came back to God that morning. They heard a message on forgiveness and reconciliation that convicted them both right down to their toes. They went forward at the end of the service and knelt together at the altar. They cried out to God. They prayed for His forgiveness and His help. God heard them and answered. They told me that they now had hope that they could rebuild their marriage.

I spent three months in therapy with Steve and Debbie. They had a lot of difficult, painful work to do. They talked through the affairs. They cleaned out all their resentments. They grieved together the loss of the dream of a healthy son. They dedicated themselves to work as a team in the treatment of their son. They learned to communicate, to resolve conflicts, and to love each other again. But through it all, one person gave them the strength to save their relationship—God Himself. With God's presence and help, Steve and Debbie did their work in therapy and began the healing process. They forged an incredibly strong spiritual bond, and it was that bond that got them through. They're still married, and they're doing well.

Quite a story, isn't it? And all of it is true. Even though Steve and Debbie faced events more difficult and stressful than most couples, all marriage partners go through tough times. Have you ever been in a situation so desperate and painful that you weren't sure your marriage could survive it? Some of you have been. Some of you may be in one right now. Some of you have yet to face a real crisis.

Storms will hit every marriage. Perseverance and trust in God not only carry you through crises, but they can also fuse a spiritual bond between you and your spouse.

## YOUR MARRIAGE MUST BE TESTED

The Bible teaches that trials test and strengthen our faith in God as individuals. James wrote:

Consider it all joy, my brethren, when you encounter various trials, knowing that the testing of your faith produces endurance. And let endurance have its perfect result, that you may be perfect and complete, lacking in nothing. (James 1:2–4)

Paul echoed James's message when he described the suffering every Christian can expect to experience:

We are afflicted in every way, but not crushed; perplexed, but not despairing; persecuted, but not forsaken; struck down, but not destroyed.... Therefore we do not lose heart, but though our outer man is decaying, yet our inner man is being renewed day by day. (2 Corinthians 4:8–9, 16)

The trials we go through are an essential part of the sanctification process. They help us grow up in Christ. James tells us that trials lead to perseverance and spiritual maturity. According to Paul, trials produce spiritual renewal. I want these qualities, and the Bible says I can get them only through suffering. That's not the way I would choose to grow and mature, but that's the way God says it happens.

Just as trials test and strengthen an individual's faith, they do the same for marriages. If our *collective* faith in God is to grow, it must undergo testing. If we are to develop the kind of marriage God wants us to enjoy, we will have to go through hardships. I believe that it's God's plan that weathering storms is the way we gain perseverance, spiritual maturity, and spiritual renewal in our relationships. A godly, intimate marriage is forged and shaped through times of stress, difficulty, and conflict.

## Crisis Is Painful but Necessary

If there's one thing I've learned as a clinical psychologist, it's that marriages change the most when there's a crisis. Oh, marriages can change to some degree when things are going smoothly. Couples can make minor adjustments and reach understandings. But it usually takes a crisis to bring serious, deep, and lasting changes.

Couples don't come to see me and say, "Dave, everything's going smoothly, but we really want to work hard and make our marriage even better." One time—just one time—I want to hear those words. When couples come to me, they're usually in a big mess. Their marriages have been blown apart by a crisis, and the pieces are scattered everywhere.

As a matter of fact, a crisis can work wonders in a marriage. It can:

- open up a man who won't talk or express love;
- bring a non-Christian partner to Christ;
- bring a carnal partner back to Christ;
- get rid of old, entrenched, destructive patterns of behavior;
- create new, healthy patterns;
- turn a so-so marriage into a passionate, intimate one;
- begin the healing of a sexual addiction;
- stop domestic violence.

I could go on and on. You name the marriage problem; a crisis can initiate a cure—at least, potentially. I say potentially because I firmly believe that what a crisis in a marriage is all about is spiritual intimacy. God allows it so that we'll reach a deeper level of spiritual bonding. None of these changes—in fact, no real relationship change at all—will happen without spiritual bonding.

If you seize the opportunity in a crisis to spiritually bond, you can solve any marital problem. Whatever needs changing can be changed. Whatever needs healing can be healed. Why? Because it will be the two of you and God against the problems. No problem is too big for God.

A crisis can also horribly wound and kill a marriage. I see that happen often. It all depends on how you and your spouse choose to handle it—on your own or with God.

## HOW PAIN DEEPENS SPIRITUAL INTIMACY

This is a difficult thing to write, and I don't do it lightly: One of the main ways to deepen your spiritual intimacy as a couple is by struggling through a crisis with God. There are five reasons why this is so.

First, *you and your partner will be totally dependent on God.* Your situation is a mess, and you have no choice but to run to God and cling to Him. You're just like little children who are overwhelmed by hurt and want to be in their daddy's arms. God desires this kind of dependence, and He will welcome you both and draw you to Himself. You will feel His comfort, support, and love.

Second, *you will see God up close and personal.* You'll both pray together as you've never prayed before. You'll listen to God as you've never listened before. You'll witness God reaching out and touching you with His guidance, strength, and compassion. You'll look on in amazement as He personally moves and works in your painful circumstances. It is, quite possibly, the closest you will ever get on earth to God's presence.

Third, *your relationship will be purified.* The pain strips away sinful patterns that have plagued your marriage for years. Crisis forces you to change by making both of you keep your eyes on God. With your focus on God, you won't repeat old patterns, and they'll die from neglect. With your focus on God, you and your partner will become more like Him, and when you're more like God, you are automatically closer to Him and to each other.

Fourth, *you will face the pain together.* It's the three of you— God, your partner, and you—against the crisis. Fighting a common enemy always strengthens the relationship among the soldiers on the front line. When your platoon of three wins the battle, your allegiance and connection to your heavenly leader will be greatly strengthened.

Finally, *your spiritual commitment to each other will be solidified.* When you weather the storm and come out with a better marriage, you both will praise God in a heartfelt and powerful way. You know that He saved you, and you won't forget it. The crisis will serve as a memorial to God's grace and provision for your marriage. And every time you look back and praise God for what He did, you'll energize your spiritual intimacy just a little bit more.

## HOPE IS WHERE GOD IS

The answer for Steve and Debbie, and for you and your partner, is in the Bible. The answer to all of life's problems, and all of marriage's problems, is in the Bible. In times of terrible pain and crisis, there's only one person who can help you.

> The righteous cry and the LORD hears,
> And delivers them out of all their troubles.
> The LORD is near to the brokenhearted,
> And saves those who are crushed in spirit. (Psalm 34:17–18)

> He will call upon Me,
> And I will answer him; I will be with him in trouble;
> I will rescue him, and honor him. (Psalm 91:15)

> Come to Me, all who are weary and heavy-laden,
> and I will give you rest. (Matthew 11:28)

> In Me you may have peace. In the world you have
> tribulation, but take courage; I have overcome the
> world. (John 16:33)

If you cry out to God, He'll answer you. He'll come, and He'll help. It's a promise—a guarantee. God is just waiting for you to ask. So why aren't you asking? Because you're selfish, stubborn, and bound and determined to handle it your way.

Your marriage is torn to bits. It's over. To put it back together you face work that is literally overwhelming. You don't have the motivation, the energy, or the skills. It's like standing at the foot of Mount Everest with a small garden spade and being told, "Start digging and level out this ground." But God can do the impossible, and He will do it—*if* you both turn to Him.

God loves it when you finally stop relying on your own puny strength and turn to Him. You need to admit that your situation is hopeless. Very often, that's how spiritual bonding starts in the life of a married couple. With God's help and power, you can work through the stages of recovery. Along the way, you create a spiritual bond…which is the whole point of the crisis! Your growing spiritual intimacy will get your marriage through it, and it will give you the intimate relationship you've always wanted. And when the next crisis comes, the three of you—God, your spouse, and you—will be ready.

## THE WAY OUT

There is a process you need to go through to completely heal from a traumatic event in your marriage. It's difficult, and it takes time. But with God's help, you and your partner can negotiate the five stages of recovery. Here's a brief overview of the stages.

### Face the Pain

The two of you must directly face exactly what happened. Too many couples try to sidestep the pain and move past it quickly. This never works. The pain remains and chokes the life out of their marriage. You must talk about the event, over and over, in order to begin your healing. The details are important because they unlock the door to your internal pain. Attached to the details are all the anguished, destructive emotions that must be expressed.

The only way I got Steve to feel his pain about his autistic son was through the details of his birth, early life, and continuing struggles. I encouraged Steve and Debbie to look at and talk through every painful milestone and setback in their son's life. Finally, after a few sessions, Steve broke, and tears flowed. His wall had come down.

### Feel and Express the Pain

Once you face and accept your pain, you have to vent it—over and over and over. The anger, rage, hurt, sadness, bitterness all have to come out, like waves crashing against the shore. It may take weeks or months for you to totally cleanse your system of painful emotions. Direct them at those who hurt you: a spouse, a child, a friend, yourself.

God may be on your list, too. You know that He allowed the difficult event. He can take your strongest emotions. Prayer is essential in this stage. You need to pray together as much as possible. Cry out to God. Don't hold back. Wrestle in prayer in the way that Paul said Epaphras prayed (see Colossians 4:12). These ought to be intense, gut-wrenching prayer sessions.

I gave Debbie permission to vent about Steve's two affairs. This didn't make me too popular with Steve, but it was for his own good. She blasted him again and again, each time releasing a little more of the pain stored in her heart. I also allowed her to ask questions about the affairs (with the exception of the sexual details, since that wouldn't do any good). Steve's job was to be kind, patient, and loving in the face of Debbie's torrent of pain and questions. Every time that he handled her with gentleness was a healing moment. We followed the same process for her affair.

### Get All the Resentment Out

Something most people don't understand is that you have to face more than just the pain connected to the traumatic event. The current trauma will trigger all the unresolved resentments in the history of the relationship. They all have to come out, or genuine healing will not occur. That's bad news, because it increases the amount of pain significantly. That's also good news, because it's God's method of helping you as a couple clear out all your emotional baggage in one massive purge so you can truly bury the past and start over.

In addition to dealing with their affairs, Steve and Debbie had to flush out many old, stuffed resentments against each other. These painful events triggered memories of all the times they had hurt each other over the course of their marriage. They had never expressed these hurts in a healthy way, and it had to be done. With each memory or incident, they were able to release their pent-up emotions in a Christlike way.

## Forgive

In God's system of trauma recovery, everything leads to forgiveness. After you have faced, felt, and expressed your pain and resentments, it's time to choose to forgive. You accept what God has allowed to happen, and you forgive all those who hurt you so deeply. You will have to trust God for allowing the trauma. You come back to Him. You begin to restore your relationship with Him. You have renewed hope for your marriage.

Forgiveness isn't easy. In fact, sometimes it seems impossible. Only with God's power can you forgive. Debbie had to forgive Steve, and Steve had to forgive Debbie. How could they forgive each other and trust again? It had to be God doing it for them. The only way they could possibly forgive was to embrace Jesus, the sinless Savior who died to forgive *their* sins.

## Build a New Marriage

The fifth and final stage involves creating a brand-new marriage. You learn new skills: how to communicate, enjoy each other, meet needs, resolve conflicts, and understand male-female differences.

But the centerpiece, the foundation of your new relationship, is your *spiritual intimacy*. Your *spiritual bond* got you through the crisis, and now it's going to power the rest of your married life.

## God Is Still in the Miracle Business

Do you wonder if God is still in the miracle business? I don't. I see miracles every week. They may not happen instantaneously, but they're miracles all the same. I could tell you hundreds of stories about every conceivable crisis that threatens to destroy marriages: adultery, homosexuality, sexual addiction, childhood sexual abuse, alcoholism, drug use, domestic violence, financial ruin, depression, loss of a child, and on and on. In every case, those who survived did so only with God's help.

I told you Steve and Debbie's story because it seemed so overwhelmingly hopeless at first. I don't understand the kind of faith Steve and Debbie demonstrated. I am awed by it. What I do understand is that this kind of faith comes only from God. Their marriage appeared to be absolutely over. But, amazingly, it survived! They not only survived, they came out stronger. God Himself spiritually renewed their marriage.

Take heart and take hope. If this couple can make it, you and your spouse can make it, too.

PART FOUR

OVERCOMING THE

BARRIERS TO

SPIRITUAL

INTIMACY

# 20

# "MY SPOUSE COULD CARE LESS!"

⁂

*The Top Ten Ways to Motivate Your Mate to Spiritually Bond*

've just finished a presentation on spiritual intimacy in marriage, and two ladies are waiting to talk to me. They introduce themselves and tell me that they are good friends. One lady speaks for both of them: "Dr. Clarke, we want to spiritually bond with our husbands. It's the desire of our hearts! We really like your approach and believe that your ideas would make all the difference in our marriages. But my husband isn't a Christian. My friend Janie's husband is a Christian, but he won't even talk about spiritual things. How can we begin this process if our husbands don't want to join us?" I've had this same conversation with many wives (and some husbands) during my weekend marriage seminars and in my office.

The bad news is that one of the main obstacles to spiritual bonding is a spouse who's not interested. Perhaps your mate is not a Christian and therefore cannot spiritually bond. Or maybe your spouse is a Christian but just doesn't want to develop the spiritual part of your relationship. Either way, you're stuck and unable to experience the deepest intimacy possible in marriage.

The good news is that there are a number of practical, effective things you can do to motivate your spouse in the area of spiritual intimacy. Over the last few years, I've developed a list of the top ten ways to draw a spouse into spiritual bonding. Whatever your situation—trying to lead your partner to Christ or trying to get your Christian partner to spiritually bond with you—these same steps apply. If you follow them, you'll be doing the best you can to influence your spouse.

For three reasons, I'm writing this chapter to a wife who is trying to motivate a husband. First, a woman is more likely to be reading this book. Second, far more women than men feel the need to spiritually bond. Third, I want to avoid the awkward use of "he/she" and "husband/wife." Obviously, there are plenty of husbands who need help attracting their wives to the spiritual bonding process, and most of the principles can be used with women, too.

## 1. PRESENT YOUR CASE

When you first bring up the issue of spiritual bonding with your husband, your approach must be logical and practical. As I mentioned previously, most men do not respond to emotion. He probably will not respond to any direct, forceful approach. If he feels that you are pressuring him, he'll get his back up, and you'll face a wall of resistance. You may express your emotions, but it's best to do so in a low-key, nonthreatening way.

You must also avoid any hint that you feel you are spiritually superior or a more knowledgeable Christian. If he feels the least bit inferior, his defenses will go up, and your chances of success will go down.

Before you even broach the subject, you must understand that he won't respond right away. You know that, don't you? He won't say, "Honey, great idea! I wish I'd thought of this spiritual bonding stuff myself. Let's do it. Take my hand, and let's pray right now." There are perhaps five men in the entire world who would respond this way, and you're probably not married to one of them. Men, by nature, have a delayed reaction to serious, deep subjects.

Tell your husband that you want to discuss something important with him. Make him wait a day or two, so he knows it's something big. Then sit down and ask him to listen and hear you out. Tell him that you don't want him to respond now (not that he would, anyway). This makes him feel in control and gives him time to process what you've said.

Present your case for spiritual bonding in a simple, straightforward, and brief way. Do not go over fifteen minutes. Cover the benefits: It will help us grow spiritually as individuals; it will create physical and emotional intimacy in our marriage; and it will lead to God's blessing. Tell him that your marriage is not what it could be. It's missing something. You've read a wonderful book by a top Christian psychologist, and you've realized that spiritual intimacy is what's missing.

What you're doing is creating in him a need for spiritual intimacy. You're not inventing his need. It's there. You're just trying to get the man to see it.

If you're struggling with a specific problem in your marriage, bring it up in this initial conversation. Tell your husband that putting God at the center of your relationship is the key to solving the problem. With God, you can solve anything.

Finish your opening statement by asking him to think and pray about what you've said. Ask him to give you a response when he's ready. There's a high likelihood that he will not get back to you. Or, if he does, he won't be willing yet to lead in a spiritual bonding process. What you've done is to clearly state the need, establish spiritual bonding as a priority, and set the stage for my nine other strategies.

## 2. Be a Dynamic Christian

Model a Spirit-filled, vibrant, Christian life. (Obviously, this should be genuine and not just a ploy.) Let your husband witness your joy in Christ. Your spouse won't be interested in Christ if your spiritual life is blah. If it doesn't work for you, what makes you think he will want it? You are the best advertisement for a relationship with Jesus that your husband will ever see.

The Bible teaches that it is possible to win a spouse to Christ without even saying a word. You can't make a person want to be spiritual, but you can draw your non-Christian or spiritually apathetic spouse to Christ by exhibiting a spirituality that is alive and authentic (see 1 Corinthians 7 and 1 Peter 3).

Let him see you meeting regularly with God for personal prayer, Bible study, and devotions. If you have children, lead family devotions at least once a week. Invite him, but hold the family meetings even if your husband refuses to attend or is opposed to them. Every night, pray with each child before bedtime.

Even if your spouse will not go with you, attend church every week with the kids. Go even if he discourages you from going or tells you flatly not to go. Some well-meaning Christian wives allow their non-Christian husbands to prevent them from attending church. They say that they are obeying the Bible's admonition to be submissive and live in harmony with others. I say baloney. You have a higher law to obey. God wants every Christian to be part of a local church body.

You need to worship God with others. Your children need to learn how to walk with Jesus. You need spiritual teaching and interaction with others who love the Lord. It's also a good idea to join a women's Bible study. Your church might have one, or you could join an excellent parachurch ministry such as Bible Study Fellowship. It's hard—incredibly hard—to live with a man who's not leading you spiritually, and you need the support that a church and Bible study group can give you.

### 3. SPIRITUALLY BOND WITH A FRIEND

Find a good friend of your same gender, a fellow Christian, with whom you can spiritually bond. The two of you can follow many of the steps outlined in the preceding chapters. Prayer together, worship, reading of God's Word, accountability, and spiritual conversations will be a source of tremendous encouragement and support. And don't forget venting. From time to time, you'll need to ask this person to listen as you "dump" the accumulated emotions that come with living with a spiritually dead or disinterested spouse. (Be careful, though—there's a thin line between genuinely expressing your emotions and bad-mouthing your spouse.) As a practical matter, there will be times when this spiritual friendship is the only thing that keeps you going.

Bonding with a close friend will enrich your own personal spiritual life. You cannot experience significant spiritual growth alone. No one can. We all have a need to spiritually bond with someone. If it can't be with your spouse, for the time being it will have to be with a same-sex friend.

### 4. SHARE YOUR SPIRITUAL LIFE WITH HIM

Ask your husband if it's okay for you to share your spiritual life with him periodically. Assure him that it will take only five minutes once or twice a week and that all he has to do is listen. You're not looking for a response (of course, you'd love one, but you're not going to ask for it). Tell him that your spiritual life is an integral part of you and that you'll feel closer to him if you can share it. Tell him that you need this. Men like to be needed. It's a rare man who will refuse this reasonable request.

Share how God is guiding and teaching you. Reveal spiritual triumphs and disappointments. Mention what you're praying for, and tell him God's answers to your prayers. Don't let his apparent lack of interest discourage you. Ignore it entirely, and continue as though he were interested. Keep on letting him see—in small glimpses—what God is doing in your life. Speak only about yourself—your feelings and experiences. Don't ask him questions, and don't try to elicit a response from him.

Your brief spiritual updates will expose him to God and what He is doing in your life. He'll become more aware of God's presence. It may draw him closer to you and to God. You are also modeling how to live for Christ and how to talk spiritually. He might just catch on and want to get more involved with you.

## 5. Tell Him What He's Missing

The average husband is satisfied with far less intimacy in his marriage than his wife is. Your husband is probably like this. He thinks everything's fine—just peachy keen. And you're dying inside. He doesn't realize how important spiritual bonding is. He just doesn't get it. To help him get it, you have to upset his comfortable, "we're doing okay" attitude about the marriage. He needs to know what you are missing—and what he's missing.

Tell him when you see God working in his life: "Jim, I think God's talking to you through that situation at work." Point out how Christ can help him in difficult times: "You don't have to face this alone—God promises to always be with us." Use examples from the lives of friends and neighbors to illustrate spiritual truths. "God really saved the Smiths' marriage. Sally told me that their faith pulled them through that hard time." Let him know how much better your marriage could be with spiritual bonding. "I think we'd have a much closer relationship if we prayed together."

Be sure not to say these things in a mean or sarcastic way. Be honest and gentle and humble. Your attitude should be one of longing on his behalf, but especially of sadness and disappointment for him. You know that his life, and your marriage, could be so much better with spiritual intimacy. So you continue to be the best wife you can be, but you don't pretend that you are completely satisfied and fulfilled.

Also, don't make these comments frequently. You don't want

to be a pest. Pick the occasions as God guides. Just say a sentence or two, and then drop it and move on.

## 6. EXPRESS YOUR FEELINGS AND DESIRES

It is essential to tell your husband periodically how you feel about the fact that you do not share Christ as a couple or enjoy spiritual intimacy. Because of that, you tell him that you feel a sense of longing, loss, and grief.

If you stuff these emotions, they will turn into frustration, bitterness, and resentment. You will pull back emotionally, and possibly physically, from your partner. You will react in anger to small mistakes your partner makes. The growing resentment inside will begin breaking you down physically, emotionally, and spiritually. As time goes on, you will entertain thoughts of leaving the marriage.

To prevent these reactions and remain committed to your marriage partner, you must clean your system from time to time by expressing your emotions. As Scripture teaches, you need to "speak the truth in love" directly to your partner (see Ephesians 4:15–27). You don't make a scene. You don't lose control, yell, or put pressure on your spouse. When you feel these painful emotions building up inside, write a letter that honestly and gently releases your pain. Here is a letter written by a wife to her non-Christian husband:

Dear Bob,

As you know, from time to time I need to write you this kind of letter. It helps me release my emotions and stay close to you.

My faith in God is such an important part of my life. I know you don't understand it, but I really could not live without God. I feel hurt, angry, and sad, because we cannot share a bond in Christ. I'm sorry for the way I acted last week. I get too intense sometimes and think I can force you to believe in Jesus and who He is and what He did for you.

I love you for who you are, and I'm thankful for the good things in our relationship. I just can't help my desire for us to add the spiritual part to our marriage so we can *truly* be one, completely.

Well, I'm done. Please don't feel you have to respond to this letter. I hope you don't feel pressured by it. If and when you trust Christ, it will have to be your decision.

Thanks for having patience with me. I love you.

Cindy

If you have a Christian husband, you'll follow the same approach, but your letters will focus on your intense longing for this spiritual dimension to be added to the marriage. You may express your feelings verbally if you want. A letter is easier, less threatening to the man, and still gets the job done.

Whether you talk or write, this is one-way communication. As you can see in my sample letter, you make it clear that he doesn't have to respond. In addition to washing away your painful emotions, this one-way technique keeps the issue of spiritual bonding before him. He is faced again and again with your need in this area.

## 7. Ask for Small Steps

Don't make the mistake of asking him to do too much, too soon. Spiritual bonding is hard for a man. He may not take a major role in the bonding for some time. He certainly will not lead right away. It's easy to overwhelm your husband and make him feel inadequate. Don't do that.

Here's what you do. Ask him for small steps—baby steps—as you begin the process. Tell him that *you* would like to pray, and look to him for an indication that that's fine with him. If he's okay with it, pray for a minute or two. Ask him to pray briefly with you before a date or just before the church worship service begins. Ask him to pray for thirty seconds with you about whatever he'd like to bring up. If he asks what he can pray for, smile and say: "Thank God for your beautiful wife whom you love so very much."

When the man makes the smallest move toward spiritual intimacy, praise him for it. Your immediate and heartfelt appreciation will reinforce the behavior and build his confidence. It's not quite like training a seal, but it's close. Give him affection, notes, or a special dinner. After he's carried out a small spiritual bonding behavior, tell him, "I feel closer to you" or "When you join me in our prayer time, my respect for you just climbs." These are true statements, and he needs to hear them. It is also a great reinforcement for you to mention in the presence of others something he has done when you have been doing some spiritual bonding exercises.

Also, assure him that you're pleased with progress and any step in the right direction. Tell him you're not expecting him to be Billy Graham. Let him know that you certainly don't have all the answers—that you want to work on your spiritual intimacy together.

## 8. SURROUND HIM WITH CHRISTIANS

Build relationships with Christians, and do your best to expose your husband to these godly people. Invite Christian couples from your church to your home, especially those who have children the same ages as yours. Find men who are walking with Jesus and doing at least some spiritual bonding with their wives. Ask these men to invite your husband to play golf, attend a sporting event, come to men's ministry events at the church, or go to a Promise Keepers event.

Your children can also be a great example to their dad. As you nurture the spiritual lives of your kids, your husband is bound to notice the changes. Their lives will speak volumes about Jesus. Involve the children in church programs—Sunday school, AWANA, Pioneer clubs, and youth group. Have the kids ask Dad to help them with their spiritual lessons and projects. One woman Sandy and I know had her kids recite their memory verses to her non-Christian husband. It's impossible not to be affected by your children quoting God's Word. God has promised that His Word will not return to Him without accomplishing what He desires (Isaiah 55:11).

## 9. Use Times of Crisis and Pain

When times of crisis strike your marriage and family—and they will—seize those moments to help your husband see his need for Christ and/or spiritual bonding. He will be most open to change when life is at its most painful. In these tough times, ask him to join you in prayer. If he refuses, go ahead and—in front of him— cry out to God for guidance, healing, strength, and comfort. As your spouse sees you broken and reaching out to God, he may begin to comfort you. And in doing so, he may for the first time feel a spiritual bond with you and the Lord.

## 10. Pray

Pray regularly for your spouse. Pray on your own. Pray with your spiritual bonding partner. Pray at Bible studies. Pray at church with two or three others. Ask others you know and trust to pray for your spouse. Never underestimate the power of prayer. Never give up. Never stop praying.

The thread woven throughout these ten ideas is to *live out your faith*. As you grow in your own relationship with God, your husband will notice. He'll recognize your deeper level of love, your increased patience, and your acts of kindness. It does no good to try to manipulate, coerce, or badger someone into spiritual intimacy. It won't work. The most effective way to interest a spouse in spiritual matters is to be so attractive in the way you live your life that he simply must have what you have.

# BREAKING THROUGH THE ROADBLOCKS

*Let Nothing Stand in Your Way*

The path to every significant achievement in life is full of roadblocks. Think of all the valuable, prized goals you have reached in your life: a college diploma, a graduate degree, building a business, getting a promotion, giving birth, raising a healthy family, buying a new home, growing spiritually, beating an addiction…. Remember how hard you had to work to get to the finish line? Remember the obstacles, both internal and external, that you had to get past before you could claim victory? It's probably true that the more important the goal was, the more obstacles you encountered.

Because spiritual intimacy is the most important goal you can reach in your marriage, you can expect to face some stiff opposition along the way. As I've presented my spiritual intimacy program over the past few years—both in my office and at speaking engagements—I've heard couples give many reasons why they can't follow my suggestions. In fact, I've developed a list of the *seven main obstacles* that couples face in their efforts to become joined in Christ.

I understand these seven obstacles very well because they are the same ones Sandy and I struggled through in our quest for spiritual oneness. Some of them still crop up from time to time. Knowing what these obstacles are will help you and your spouse defeat them.

## THE DEVIL'S SCHEMES

The first obstacle is the devil. You are in a war—a brutal, vicious, spiritual war with the powers of hell. The sooner you realize that, the sooner you can get prepared. God has given us plenty of warning in the Bible:

> Be self-controlled and alert. Your enemy the devil prowls around like a roaring lion looking for someone to devour. (1 Peter 5:8, NIV)

> For our struggle is not against flesh and blood, but against the rulers, against the powers, against the world forces of this darkness, against the spiritual forces of wickedness in the heavenly places. (Ephesians 6:12)

Satan hates your marriage, and he wants to destroy it. Destroying your relationship is near the top of his to-do list every day. His very name means *adversary*. He knows that spiritual bonding is the wellspring of a successful, God-honoring marriage. He knows that he can't kill your love if you keep God at the center of your lives and relationship. You better believe that he'll do everything in his power to stop you from spiritually bonding.

So what's the answer to defeating your implacable enemy? How do you and your spouse fight Satan and win? By putting God on your marital team—by making Him the head of your marriage. As James 4:7–8 tell us, "Submit therefore to God. Resist the devil and he will flee from you. Draw near to God and He will draw near to you."

When you spiritually bond, you draw near to God. When God is with you, Satan doesn't have a chance to murder your marriage. If it's you and your spouse against Satan, you'll lose every time. If it's you and your spouse *and God* against Satan, you'll win every time. All you have to do is make a simple introduction: "Satan, meet God. I think you know Him."

## "My Spiritual Life Is Personal"

As I said earlier, many people use the rationale that their faith is a private matter, not open to scrutiny or examination. They insist that they don't need to discuss the details of their spiritual life with anyone, including their spouses.

God doesn't agree. He wants you to share your spiritual life with your mate. You share in other of the most intimate ways. You should share this most important aspect. If you hold back, you will never experience the deepest level of intimacy. Your partner will never know the real you. The two of you cannot become "one flesh."

Keep in mind that you don't have to reveal all your spiritual secrets immediately. It's a slow, steady progression, which takes place as you practice the bonding behaviors.

## "It's a Never-Ending Bible Study!"

Some people have the idea that spiritual bonding will take over their whole lives. They think that they'll have to sit around all day praying, reading the Bible, and talking about spiritual things. Actually, I could think of worse things. But realistically, there is more to life than spiritual bonding. Though the effects of bonding will permeate your lives like a wonderful fragrance, it doesn't go on constantly.

There are some obnoxious people who spiritualize everything and have no other interests of any kind. I'm not recommending that. Spiritual bonding behaviors ought to become a natural, regular part of your relationship. On average, they'll take a little over one hour per week. One hour! Is this asking for the moon? You spend more time than that in the shower!

## "I'm Threatened" ("I Feel Threatened")

Many of my clients, especially men, try this excuse on me: "Dave, my partner is more mature spiritually, and that threatens me." I tell them that I understand but that it's no reason to avoid developing the spiritual part of their marriages. I ask them if they've ever felt threatened in their jobs. All reply that they have. I ask if the threat caused them to quit their jobs. They almost all respond by saying no, it didn't. Their job was important, so they overcame their feelings of being threatened. That's when I lower the boom by asking them one simple question: "What's more important— your job or your marriage?"

Yes, it can be intimidating and scary to think of connecting spiritually with a partner who has been a Christian longer than you have, has more Bible knowledge than you do, or is more advanced in the Christian life. But don't let that stop you! The fact is that you and your partner will never be at the same spiritual level. All that matters is that each of you is growing spiritually.

If you're a man who feels threatened by all this spiritual intimacy talk, express this fear or uncomfortable feeling to your partner. Get it out, and I'll bet she'll be kind and reassuring. It'll impress her that, even though you feel threatened, you're going to spiritually bond anyway. She won't say, "You ought to feel threatened, buddy. I am more advanced, and I plan to stay that way!" Instead, she'll say: "Thanks for telling me that. I know it's hard. It's hard for me, too. Let's do it together."

## "Sorry, No Time"

I won't take up a lot of space dealing with this lame excuse. You always make time for the activities you want to do. Ever noticed that? If you found out today that you had cancer, I'm fairly sure you would make the time to see your doctor and get treatments.

If you didn't, you'd die. I'm telling you that if you don't carve out the time to spiritually bond, your marriage will die.

Spiritual bonding doesn't take that much time. I have four children at home, a busy therapy practice, and a full speaking schedule. And I can make the time. If I can do it, you can do it.

## "Spiritual Bonding Isn't That Important"

If I haven't convinced you by now of the importance and superlative benefits of spiritual bonding, I guess I never will. I pray that God will help you realize that spiritual intimacy ought to be the number one priority in your marriage. It's not an option. It's not a nice bonus. It's the heart and soul of intimacy between a man and a woman. Becoming one flesh is God's design for marriage. It's the only plan He has. You either do your marriage your way or His way. Which way do you think is better?

## "I Can't Be That Vulnerable"

There's no doubt about it: Spiritual bonding requires vulnerability. Spiritual sharing is the deepest level of communication. Nothing else even comes close. It lets your spouse see the most important and personal part of your life. Being this vulnerable is very difficult. It is a risk, but it is a risk you need to take.

Don't play it safe as so many married couples do! You'll both lose. You'll have, at best, a stable and boring marriage.

You need to risk. You need to go for it.

Denise Hall, a dear friend of Sandy's and mine and someone who knows all about risks, gave me this anonymous quote printed on a beautiful, framed plaque:

RISKS
To laugh is to risk appearing the fool.
To weep is to risk appearing sentimental.
To reach out for another is to risk involvement.
To expose feelings is to risk exposing your true self.

To place your ideas, your dreams before a crowd is to
  risk their loss.
To love is to risk not being loved in return.
To live is to risk dying.
To hope is to risk despair.
To try is to risk failure.
But risks must be taken, because the greatest hazard in
  life is to risk nothing.
The person who risks nothing does nothing, has noth-
  ing, and is nothing.
They may avoid suffering and sorrow but they cannot
  learn, feel, change, grow, love, live—
Chained by their certitudes they are slaves—they have
  forfeited their freedom.
Only a person who risks is free.

The risks you take in spiritual bonding will pay off. There is
a guarantee! It's God's guarantee. *God* will not fail to bless you and
bring you and your partner as close as a couple can possibly get.
*God* will revolutionize your marriage. *God* will give you a vibrant,
stimulating, and passionate love that will last a lifetime.

I know I have covered a lot of ground in this book. Please don't
feel overwhelmed. Let me assure you that no married couple
spiritually bonds in all of these ways every week. That would be
impossible.

*Just pick a few bonding activities and begin to do them.* Start
small and build slowly. With God's help, you'll gather momen-
tum and excitement. It won't be long before it becomes a natural
part of your life together.

Some weeks you'll do more in the spiritual area; other weeks,
less. There's an ebb and flow, depending on a number of factors.
In stress and crisis, you'll spend more time together with God. In

busy periods (travel, work demands, vacations, sickness in a family member), you'll struggle to make time to bond spiritually.

Even when you get to the point where you're bonding on a regular basis, it doesn't take that much time. Sandy and I spend a little over one hour per week in the seven areas of spiritual bonding. That's not much when you consider what you get in return.

I've given you the tools you need to develop spiritual intimacy. Now it's up to you. I know you can do it! Let nothing stand in your way! I know that you and your mate will experience the same joy, peace, and power that Sandy and I have gained by growing closer to God in a spiritual bond. You can truly have a marriage after God's own heart.

# A SPIRITUAL INTIMACY CHECKLIST

Here, in list form, are the seven steps that will help you and your spouse develop spiritual intimacy. (These were presented in detail in part 3 of this book.) If you like, photocopy these pages so you can have a reference handy all the time.

## 1. PRAYER

Pray before your talk times, problem solving, sex, and every other activity. Schedule prayer times of at least five minutes each three times a week.

## 2. ONCE-A-WEEK SPIRITUAL EVALUATION MEETINGS

This includes a longer prayer time, Bible reading and study, spiritual conversation, accountability, and worship.

## 3. BIBLE READING AND STUDY

These activities should occur during three meetings over a two-week period and should cover four steps: Read, meditate, discuss, and apply a verse or passage.

## 4. SPIRITUAL CONVERSATIONS

Be intentional about including God and spiritual matters in your conversations. This should happen spontaneously, but these discussions can also be planned for specific times: before and after prayer, during your daily talk times, and at your once-a-week spiritual evaluation meeting.

## 5. ACCOUNTABILITY

Ask each other tough questions every week during your spiritual evaluation meeting.

## 6. PRIVATE WORSHIP

This should happen at least once a month.

## 7. SERVICE

The two of you—*together*—should volunteer your time, energy, and talents for ongoing or periodic service opportunities.

# SUGGESTED PLANS
# FOR SPIRITUAL BONDING

These plans begin very simply and escalate in their requirement of time, energy, and commitment. None of these plans, however, is overly time consuming or burdensome. I suggest that you and your spouse begin at whichever level you feel comfortable and move on to the next plan when you're ready. Also, these plans are just to get you started. I'm sure you'll want to tailor a plan to fit your needs and style.

## PLAN A

If this whole spiritual intimacy discussion is new to you, or if your marriage is in crisis, keep it simple at the outset. To start:

- Schedule a weekly time to pray together. Agree on how long you will pray, or leave it open. Reread the "Miracle of Prayer" narrative about the couple in the "hopeless" situation (chapter 11). Also, let the section "Pray Like Children" (chapter 13) guide you. If it feels awkward at first, that's okay. Keep going—persevere! Although it may seem difficult to do, taking this one step could save your marriage.

## PLAN B

If the ideas in this book seem feasible to you, but you and your spouse haven't been doing anything to build spiritual intimacy, begin with the following:

    ✑ Start having a weekly date night.

    ✑ When you are getting ready to leave on your date or when you arrive at your destination, hold hands, close your eyes, and pray. Thank God for each other and for the chance to have fun together.

Do this for three or four weeks. When it feels comfortable and natural, go on to the following steps:

    ✑ Sit down on Saturday or Sunday and schedule a minimum of three prayer times (five to ten minutes each) during the coming week. *Be sure to schedule a specific time and place.* These are important appointments that can help you greatly as you begin the process of spiritual bonding.

    ✑ Together, reread the sections on conversational prayer and the STORB approach (chapter 12). Try practicing this method in your three prayer times.

    ✑ Take a few minutes after each of your prayer times to read—together—chapter 15 to become familiar with "spiritual conversations."

    ✑ For as many days as you can during the week, schedule twenty to thirty minutes for private, personal, no-distractions-allowed "talk times," as suggested in chapter 15.

Get comfortable doing this, and follow the plan consistently for three months.

## PLAN C

After three months of following Plan B fairly consistently, add these steps:

- Begin adding *one* twenty- to thirty-minute "spiritual evaluation session" each week. Schedule this meeting near the end of the week. Refer to chapter 13 for more explanation.

- Purchase notebooks and begin creating prayer journals to use in this weekly meeting.

## PLAN D

Once you've mastered the steps outlined above, incorporate these:

- Every other week, add an accountability component to your spiritual evaluation session, as suggested in chapter 17.

- Early in the week—on Sunday or Monday evening—read and prepare to study a Scripture passage. Reread chapter 14 and follow the four steps (read, meditate, discuss, and apply) over a two-week period.

# OTHER BOOKS BY DAVID CLARKE

*Men Are Clams, Women Are Crowbars*
*Winning the Parenting War*

To schedule a seminar or order Dr. Clarke's books,
audio tapes, and video tapes,
please contact:

DAVID CLARKE SEMINARS

**www.davidclarkeseminars.com**

1-888-516-8844
or
Marriage & Family Enrichment Center
6505 North Himes Avenue
Tampa, Florida 33614